A Wreck upon the Ocean

STUDIES IN CORNISH LANGUAGE AND CULTURE

Volume 3

STUDIES IN CORNISH LANGUAGE AND CULTURE

Volume 3

A Wreck upon the Ocean

*Cornish Folklore in the
Age of the Industrial Revolution*

Brendan McMahon

evertype

2015

Published by Evertype, 19ᴀ Corso Street, Dundee, ᴅᴅ2 1ᴅʀ, Scotland. *www.evertype.com.*

First edition 2015. Reprinted with corrections October 2021.

A catalogue record for this book is available from the British Library.

ISBN-10 1-78201-098-X
ISBN-13 978-1-78201-098-2

ISSN 2753-1597

Typeset in Baskerville by Michael Everson.

Cover design by Michael Everson, based on "The Mermaid" by John Reinhard Weguelin (1911).

iv

Contents

Acknowledgements

Some of this material has appeared in *Tradition Today* and *An Baner Kernewek*, and acknowledgements are due to the editors of those journals.

To Tom and Quynh.

Foreword

Brendan McMahon's work may be read in several magazines and publications relating to Cornwall and Cornish Studies. I have always found him one of the most reasoned and respected voices in terms of evaluating both the folk and literary continuums of Cornwall, and in particular, where they intersect and blend. His new book offers a methodology which I attempted to explain in a 2012 article for *Cornish Studies*, in which I posited the notion of a new way of examining Celtic Literature and Folklore. This, I then termed "Celtic Materialism", which I hoped would initiate a debate about the way in which Celtic Literature and Folklore was consumed, examined and interrogated.

Only a few years later comes McMahon's work here, which is a fascinating application of some of the ideas that I wished more scholars would extol onto Cornish and Celtic Studies. The trick in essence, is that McMahon leaves behind the old "Liberal Humanist" notion of literary studies, and instead, offers us something much more grounded in the economic, political, social and religious climate in which the "text" was first developed. By choosing to examine Cornish folklore during the age of the industrial revolution, McMahon cleverly sees the irony and paradoxes of this lens. Just as Cornwall was modernizing, it became clear that unless folklorists collected tales and legends they would be lost (just as elements of Cornish-language literature and folklore had been neglected in the past). Of course, the process however, crystallized the tales into pieces of literature, which although preserving them, also partially stopped their evolution. Cornwall was not however, the only European territory going through this process. As McMahon notes here, it was quite common across a number of cultures.

The paradox of this engagement is then further revealed by McMahon when it comes to the analysis of several key narratives. In the modern era, we rarely see such perceptive scholarship on the "meaning" and "origin" of the tales, as well as an understanding of what these tales mean in the mindset of the Cornish – both at home and across the globe. It is to this aspect of the psychological importance of these folktales and their contexts that this volume really comes into its own. The author examines key tales within the tradition – not only offering observations on their industrial context, but also radical new interpretations. In this sense, we are seeing the implication of Cornish folklore in history on a scale hitherto unseen.

It is my hope that more scholars will take McMahon's lead and develop further re-examination of Cornish folklore and folktale, since the field merits treatment. *A Wreck Upon the Ocean* is a significant contribution to our understanding of Cornwall's literary and folkloric heritage.

Alan M. Kent
Probus, 2015

Introduction

The Scholars and the Peasants

Folklore collection and publication in nineteenth-century Britain was a somewhat haphazard affair. Most English counties remained unsurveyed, and story collections often waited for decades before finding a publisher; indeed Georgina Jackson's Shropshire stories never saw the light of day.[1] Consequently, though much work was done, fewer than twelve fieldwork collections were published between 1865 and 1914.[2]

Most of these collections failed to meet the standards that modern folklorists would require: verbatim renditions were rare, paraphrase and journalistic reportage frequent. But when a sceptical friend of Robert Hunt remarked, "I suppose you invented most of these stories", as he was correcting the proofs for the third edition of his *Popular Romances of the West of England* in 1881, Hunt assured him and his readers that all his stories had been gathered by him personally half a century earlier. Indeed, he claimed to have been collecting stories since his early childhood:

> sixty-eight years since; preparatory to a visit I was about to make with my mother to Bodmin, above which town many stories were told, and my purpose was to record them.[3]

---

1   For this and what follows see Dorson, Richard M. (1968). *The British Folklorists.* London, Routledge and Regan Paul, pp. 316–31.

2   This does not include Scottish and Irish collections, such as Campbell's great *Popular Tales of The West Highlands*, published in four volumes (1860–2).

3   Hunt, Robert (1881, 3rd edition). *Popular Romances of the West of England, or The Drolls, Traditions and Superstititions of Old Cornwall.* London, Chatto and Windus, p. 21.

In 1829 Hunt, setting an example to countless future collectors, set out on a ten-month walking tour of Cornwall, to gather "every existing tale of its ancient people".[4] In his role as Secretary to the Royal Cornwall Polytechnic Society he gathered stories from farmers, miners and fisherfolk in the far west, and later he even employed a postmaster to collect material on his behalf. He discovered the previously unrecorded tradition of droll-telling, which was rapidly disappearing in his own time. Drolls were long, episodic tales ("Tom and the Tinkeard" is the best surviving example), told by itinerant storytellers who adapted them to fit local situations. He also provides us with a detailed picture of Uncle Anthony James, one of the last droll tellers, and his work was the first fieldwork collection of its kind. Later he was to draw on material collected by William Bottrell, author of *Traditions and Hearthside Stories of West Cornwall*.

Partly through the work of the Grimm brothers, folktales had become associated with the revolutionary forces of romantic nationalism. They were believed by many to contain "survivals" of ancient myth, and to embody the essential characteristics of the ethnic group which produced them.[5] In 1885, Elias Lönnrot published the first edition of his epic *Kalevala*, cobbled together from the traditional poetry of Karelia which, though its authenticity has been questioned, is a powerful work which was rapidly acknowledged as Finland's national epic.[6] Lönnrot himself had been inspired by MacPherson's "Ossian", an almost entirely spurious series of "translations" of Gaelic romantic poetry, said to have been composed by a third century bard, the son of Fingal, but mostly MacPherson's own work.[7] Despite its ambiguous origins the book caught the mood of the time, and had immense influence on Goethe, Herder and the other German Romantics. It fed into the primitivist cult of the "Noble Savage" and the ideas of Rousseau, a romantic response to the non-European world, and the "Fourth World" of

4   Hunt (1881), pp.xv–xvi.
5   Zipes, J. (ed) (2000). *The Oxford Companion to Fairy Tales*. Oxford, OUP, pp. 218–19.
6   See Lönnrot, E (1989). *The Kalevala*, trans. Keith Bosley, Oxford, OUP.
7   See Drabble, M (ed) (2000, 6th edition). *Oxford Companion to English Literature*. Oxford, OUP, pp. 627–28.

minority cultures within Europe itself. This was coupled with a growing unease caused by the homogenization and environmental destruction which industralization brought in its wake.

Gathering the Fragments

Though progress was generally seen as benevolent and inescapable, a growing sense of what was being lost produced a certain unease and ambivalence, along with a desire to preserve what was passing for posterity. Hunt himself expresses something of this towards the end of his introduction:

> Romances such as these have floated down to us as wreck upon the ocean. We gather a fragment here and a fragment there, and at length it may be, we learn something of the name and character of the vessel when it was freighted with life, and obtain a shadowy image of the people who have perished.
>
> Hoping to have been successful in saving a few interesting fragments of the unwritten records of a peculiar race, my labours are submitted to the world.[8]

My own book, I should say, presumes the existence of a Cornish national community which has existed throughout historic time, including Hunt's time, into our own time and into the future. Though Cornish nationality is mocked throughout the rest of Britain, the recent recognition of it by the Council of Europe under its framework Convention for the Protection of National Minorities demonstrates its validity.[9]

Hunt's comment is typical of its time. Alongside an immense pride in their own remarkable achievements, this sense of loss was very much a part of the Victorian world-view.[10] At home and abroad folktales were associated with primitive and defeated people, who were seen through the eyes of a racist ideology, required by capitalism to justify its exploitation. They were told by simple, working class people, often servants, and dismissed as "superstition".

8   Hunt, *op. cit.*, p. 32.

9   See *Cornish Nation.* 68, Summer/Autumn 2014.

10 In the poetry of Tennyson, for instance, or Hardy's novels.

The publishers of folk stories thus found themselves in the ambivalent position of having to disparage their own texts, lest they themselves be considered "primitive" and "superstitious" by their middle-class, English target audience. On several occasions, Hunt himself welcomes the fact that education is destroying traditional belief:

> Those wild dreams which swayed with irresistible force the skin clad Briton of the Cornish hills, have not yet entirely lost their power where even the National and the British schools are busy with the people, and Mechanics Institutions are diffusing the truths of science.[11]

Early scholars of the Cornish language felt obliged to assume a similarly negative attitude towards their subject, though not all went so far as Matthew Arnold, whose *Study of Celtic Literature* led to his becoming Oxford's first Professor of Celtic:

> I must say I quite share the opinion of my brother Saxons as to the practical inconvenience of perpetuating the speaking of Welsh. It may cause a moment's distress to one's imagination when one hears that the last Cornish peasant who spoke the old tongue of Cornwall is dead; but no doubt Cornwall is the better for adopting English, for becoming more thoroughly one with the rest of the country. The fusion of all the inhabitants of these islands into one homogenous, English-speaking whole, the breaking down of barriers between us, the swallowing up of separate provincial nationalities, is a consummation to which the natural course of things irresistibly tends.[12]

That even a self-confessed "Celt-lover" could write this appalling passage tells us much about official policy towards the Celtic languages in Arnold's day down to our own.

Cornish died as a community language in the second half of the eighteenth century, and "the last Cornish peasant who spoke the old

---

11 Hunt, *op. cit.*, p. 25.

12 Arnold, M, 1910 (1867). *On the Study of Celtic Literature and Other Essays.* London, J M Dent, p. 20.

tongue" is often said, mistakenly, to be Dolly Pentreath from Mouse-hole. That it lasted so long after the dissolution of its institutions (particularly Glasney College, the source of Cornish drama), the imposition of a foreign liturgy, and the slaughter that followed the Prayer Book Rebellion, is miraculous. The precise moment when a language dies is of course difficult to pinpoint, and there is plenty of evidence for the survival of numerals, prayers, endearments and the like into the nineteenth and even twentieth century. It is often said that the first scholars learned the language from the last speakers, and it was this that allowed Henry Jenner and Robert Morton Nance to launch the language revival early in the twentieth century.[13] In Hunt's time language loss was a recent event, and the language must have been a pervasive presence still, though much of the traditional narrative of the droll-teller must have gone with the language, and as a result of the social and industrial change sweeping through the Duchy.

At the same time, and in much the same spirit, the surviving texts of Medieval Cornish literature were being gathered together, edited and published. The Passion poem, *Pascon agan Arluth*, was published and translated by Gilbert Davies in 1826; *The Creation of the World*, *'Gwreans an bys'*, edited by the great Irish scholar Whitley Stokes in 1864; Stokes' edition and translation of *Bewnans Meriasek* in 1872.[14] In 1859 Edwin Norris published the great trilogy known as the *Ordinalia*, dealing with the Passion, Death and Resurrection of Christ, the events of Easter week, the high point of the church's year.[15]

In his introduction, Norris who, like Matthew Arnold, knew scarcely any Cornish, wrote:

It will be understood, as a matter of course, that quantity and antiquity are here the chief elements of value and that,

---

13 Berresford Ellis, P (1974). *The Cornish Language and its Literature*. London, Routledge and Kegan Paul, pp. 95–124.

14 Gilbert Davies (1826). *Mount Calvary, Interpreted in the English Tongue*. London, Nichols. Stokes, W (1864). *Guireans an bys. The Creation of the World*. London, Williams and Norgate. Stokes, W (1872). *The Life of St Meriasek, Bishop and Confessor*. London, Trubner.

15 Norris, E (1859). *The Ancient Cornish Drama*. Oxford, OUP.

apart from some evidence of the condition and culture of the Cornish Celts of the fourteenth or fifteenth century, the term 'important' applies to the language only; in regard to the matter there is nothing in these dramas that may not be found in such as have been printed in English, French and Latin under the designation of mysteries, or Miracle Plays.[16]

As a matter of fact this is untrue. The Cornish plays are unique not only in their language but in their open-air staging and Cornish settings.[17] Their use of the Legend of the Rood and the subversive subtext of the saints' plays (of which more later), is also distinctive. But in fact, the idea that the dramatists might have had something to say to living men and women seems not to have occurred to Norris, to whom the plays are of no more than philological interest. For me medieval literature is the closest we have to a traditional Cornish world-view, which is why I have used it to illuminate the folktales. Of course the plays also employ the profound themes of the wider Christian world of which Cornwall was then a vibrant part, what Brian Murdoch calls "the divine economy of history", the "felix culpa" of a fall by means of a tree, which was redeemed by the tree of the Cross.[18] Norris' strictures on the literary merits of the plays are also unfounded, and, as with other scholars we have encountered, are based on racial and political assumptions. For nineteenth century English gentlemen, Cornwall had to be peripheral, and therefore its language, literature and folklore had to be marginalized. The expansion of tourism in the 1850s following the arrival of the railways made Cornish culture a commercial asset in some respects, but still the fragments had to be re-arranged to make them palatable to visitors.[19] Hence the mood shifted from the brutal triumphalism of Arnold and Norris to the more indulgent and patronizing strain of later writers, which is still with us. Cornwall is cute, but it is still not allowed to be different. As translators of the fragmented Cornish

---

16 *Ibid*, pv.

17 Murdoch, B (1993). *Cornish Literature. Cambridge*, D S Brewer, pp. 41–43.

18 *Ibid*, p. 45.

19 Deacon, B (1997). "The hollow jarring of the distant steam engines: images of Cornwall between West Barbary and Delectable Duchy", pp. 7–24. In

tradition, this placed Robert Hunt and William Bottrell (whose work Hunt drew upon) in an uncomfortable position.

Nonetheless, their work brings us closer to this branch of the Cornish tradition than we can ever be now, and it is quite clear that they regarded their material as more than whimsy to entertain tourists. For that reason, and because the relationship between narrative and context is a principal theme of this book, I have tried to retain Hunt's story categories, even though they represent ways of thinking about folklore which now seem anachronistic. Whether they represent categories which were meaningful for the droll tellers is now impossible to say, but they are more likely to correspond to important distinctions within the tradition than any categories which we might devise for ourselves. At the same time I am trying to preserve whatever may remain of a Cornish voice, a voice which was deliberately excluded by Matthew Arnold and Edwin Norris for instance.

Hunt's categories include "The Giants", "The Fairies", "The Mermaids", "Tregeagle", "The Saints", "King Arthur", and "The Miners". The remaining categories are to do with popular superstitions, ghost stories and the like which are unlikely to form part of any enduring tradition but which are, of course, always popular. There are stories (he is a good storyteller himself), which Hunt seems to tell in the manner of the then popular "novel of suspense" as written by Wilkie Collins, and this is in part an attempt to solve his "translation problem", though most of the tales are told in the more down to earth tones in which he doubtless heard them.[20] But I have also combined Hunt's categories ("The mermaid and the saint", "The lawyer and the king", and so on), partly in the hope of casting fresh light on the material, but also to bring out those qualities that suggest the integrity of Cornish folklore as a distinctive world-view and a focus of communal identity. This is particularly true of the more "traditional" material, even in detail (the "giant-

---

Westland, E (1997). *Cornwall: The Cultural Construction of Place*. Penzance, Patten Press/University of Exeter.

20 See Hughes, W (1980). *The Maniac in the Cellar: Sensation Novels of the 1860s*. New Jersey, Priceton University Press. Also Wilkie Collins. *The Woman in White* and *The Moonstone*.

like" qualities of both Arthur and Tregeagle, for instance), and one can only wonder to what extent the missing Cornish language material would have borne out this view.

Droll Tellers and Bards

It seems to me that the most important question to be asked about folktales is not where they come from, how they are disseminated or what they might tell us about long defunct belief systems, but rather how and why they were told. We don't know much about the droll tellers (though Deane and Shaw's summary is interesting),[21] but we do know that they were peripatetic tinsmiths who sang for their supper and whose songs and stories were much valued by the communities they served. Like the bards of ancient Ireland they had a fondness for scurrility and public dispute (witness the dispute between Billy Foss and Blind Dick in the early nineteenth century),[22] and one might construct a romantic picture of them as decayed bards of ancient Britain.[23] But origin is less than function, and it seems to me that these wandering storytellers helped to consolidate a community that had lost its language and its institutions, and that was being torn apart by rapid industrialization and social mobility, followed by no less rapid economic collapse and large scale emigration, and to manage the huge personal and communal losses entailed in these social processes.

Stories which are told in hard pressed communities over centuries are never merely frivolous, since that would be an unaffordable waste of time and energy. Even on the most superficial level they meet the basic human need for entertainment, social interaction and cohesion. But the stories themselves do more than this. By dealing with the tensions and conflicts that shape our lives they help us to deal with them and so these stories teem with desire and death, love and loss.[24]

21 Deane, T and Shaw, T (2003). *Folklore of Cornwall*. Stroud, Tempus Publishing, pp. 116–123.

22 *Ibid*, pp. 118–9.

23 Nagy, J F and Jones, L E (eds) (2005). *Heroic Poets and Poetic Heroes in Celtic Tradition: A Festschrift for Patrick K. Ford*. CSANA Yearbook 3–4. Dublin, Four Courts Press.

24 See Booker, C (2004). *The Seven Basic Plots: Why We Tell Stories*. London, Bloomsbury

At the moment when we first see them they are passing, but still sufficiently relevant to be passed on and collected, But, as an expression of shared memory and identity, their time was all but over.

Chapter 1

The Pixie and the Baby

I

The Historical Context

The nineteenth century was a period of unprecedented social and economic change, at least in France and England. From France emerged the possibility of political transformation, which was to have profound historical consequences, and from England the no less momentous possibility of industrial transformation, forces which combined to create a triumphant liberal capitalism which consolidated and extended its power in the latter half of the century.[1]

Britain, where much of this process began, was of course a scene of unprecedented social and industrial change at this time. Between 1831 and 1901 the population increased by ten percent in each decade, and cities grew disproportionately: when Victoria came to the throne only five towns in England and Wales had a population of more than one hundred thousand; by the end of the reign, there were twenty-three.[2] Cornwall too was transformed: the population increased from 192,000 to 322,000, though it fell during the last three decades of the century due to recession and emigration as we shall see.[3]

Cornish people played a big part in the transformation of Britain, and the wider world, and it would be hard to imagine the Industrial Revolution without Humphrey Davy, Richard Trevithick, and the

---

1   See, for instance, Hobsbawm, Eric (1962). *The Age of Revolution, 1789–1848.* London, Weidenfeld and Nicholson; and *The Age of Capital, 1848–1875* (1975). London, Weidenfeld and Nicolson.

2   Briggs, Asa (1963). *Victorian Cities.* London, Oldhams.

3   Hill, Charles Peter (1977). *British Economic and Social History 1700–1975*, 4th edition. London, Edward Arnold, p. 4.

countless Cornish engineers and miners who made the wheels turn, everywhere from Mexico to South Australia.[4] The landscape itself was changed forever. At the beginning of the century Cornwall was the world's biggest copper producer, and technological innovation caused both copper and tin production to soar; old mines were re-opened and between 1800 and 1837 the number of workings rose from seventy-five to over two hundred. The towns boomed, and the new railways connected Cornwall to the rest of Britain, providing new markets for her raw materials. But in the "Hungry Forties" crops failed, food prices rocketed, and the population began to fall back, though it remained much higher than it had been at the turn of the century. Although production (and profits) surged ahead, conditions in the mines were frightful, and the men half-starved. In spite of this, production costs rose while foreign competition grew. Many miners left for South America, or Michigan, where their descendants still argue about the proper way to make a pasty.[5] As the recession began to bite, outside interests came to control the mining industry; old, co-operative ways of working, based on a communal sense of the common good, were lost; and industrial relation deteriorated.[6] The psychological effects of all this must have been profound, and Hamilton Jenkin writes of "the bitter leave takings there must have been in those black years when the Cornish people, who still love their home after a lifetime of separation, were first called upon to leave their natural inheritance".[7]

The Victorian age was shaped by the tension between continuity and change, and the transformations were ideological as well as scientific and industrial: indeed these domains were organically linked in the social nexus. The French Revolution challenged both the ancient aristocracies of Europe and the ideologies which maintained them, and made it possible for the new middle classes

---

4 Hamilton Jenkin, A K (1927). *The Cornish Miner*. London, Allen and Unwin.
5 Lockwood, Y R and Lockwood, W G. "Pasties in Michigan's upper peninsula: foodways, inter-ethnic relations and regionalism". In Stern, S and Cicala, J A (eds) (1991). *Creative Ethnicity: Symbols and Strategies of Contemporary Ethnic Life*. Logan, Utah, Utah State University Press.
6 Lewis, J (2006). "Cornish copper mining 1795–1830", in *Cornish Studies*, 14.
7 Hamilton Jenkin (1927).

to take power. In Britain too, this was an ideological shift, since the bourgeoisie were mostly nonconformist, as opposed to the Anglican aristocracy. Since the Church controlled access to the universities and Parliament, this had serious practical implications, and effectively disenfranchised millions of citizens, including Roman Catholics and Jews. These disadvantages were gradually removed as the century wore on.

The link between social and scientific development could generate conflict: the dispute between the Darwinians and the bishops was a fight over status and funding, among other things.[8] But it did unsettle the faithful, of course, and contribute to the growing, threatening sense that the British landscape, in both the literal and the intellectual sense, was changing forever.

Many Victorians recognized the historic nature of this trans-formation and rejoiced in it. In a 1948 broadcast, the historian Humphrey House said of them:

> At one moment they are busy congratulating themselves on their brilliant achievements, at the next they are moaning about their sterility, their lack of spontaneity. In either mood they are all agog at being modern, more modern than anybody has ever been before, and in this they were right. They took the brunt of an utterly unique development of human history. The industrialization and mechanization of life meant a greater change in human capabilities in the practical sphere than ever before had been possible.[9]

Of course, liberal capitalism had its critics. Some criticism took the form of political opposition based on the revolutionary French tradition. 1848 was the year of revolutions and in 1849 Marx settled in London, where he wrote *Das Kapital*. During the second half of the century the working class began to develop its own independent organizations, and the ruling classes either liberalized (as in Britain) or came under increasing pressure. Criticism often took the form of

8   Desmond, A and Moore, J (1991). *Darwin*. London, Michael Joseph, *passim*.

9   Ford, B (ed) (1992). *Cambridge Cultural History of Britain*, Vol 7, Victorian Britain. Cambridge, Cambridge University Press, p. 17.

comparing an ugly or unjust present with an idealized rural past. Carlyle, deeply influenced by German romanticism, attacked contemporary Utilitarianism, and Ruskin's great book, *The Stones of Venice* (1851–3) began a rehabilitation of Gothic style whose monuments may still be seen all over Britain, and indeed the world.[10] Gothic architecture was championed by the Cambridge Ecclesiologists,[11] and by the extraordinary A. W. Pugin.[12] It is hard to see Pugin's "Perfect Cheadle" for instance (St Giles' remarkable Catholic church in that Staffordshire town), as anything other than a rejection of Victorian Utilitarianism, in both the aesthetic and ideological senses. Pugin's response to a modernity he detested was an attempt to recreate an idealized medieval past, much as William Morris opposed his enthusiasm for "medieval" craftsmanship against the industrial mass production of the Victorian age.[13]

The folklore collectors: Hunt and Bottrell

Against this background, folklore began to attract attention as the embodiment of a traditional wisdom that was in danger of being swept aside by the rising tide of industrialism. This was a pan-European phenomenon. The Grimms, of course, started publishing their groundbreaking stories in 1812, and Crofton Croker's Irish tales appeared in 1825.[14] As far afield as Russia, Alexander Afanasyev published hundreds of tales from 1853 on, under extremely difficult conditions.[15] In Britain similar developments led to the formation of the Folklore Society in 1878. Howells' *Cambrian Superstitions* appeared in 1831, and Campbell of Islay (Iain Òg Ìle)

10 Hunt, John Dixon (1982). *The Wider Sea: A Life of John Ruskin*. London, Dent.

11 White, James F. (1962). *The Cambridge Movement: The Ecclesiologists and the Gothic Revival*. Cambridge, Cambridge University Press.

12 Hill, Rosemary (2007). *God's Architect: Pugin and the Building of Romantic Britain*. London, Allen Lane.

13 Grennan, Margaret Rose (1945). *William Morris, Medievalist and Revolutionary*. New York, King's Crown Press.

14 Croker, T. C. (February 26 1825). "Fairy legends of traditions of the south of Ireland". Extract from *London Literary Gazette and Journal of Belles Letters*, no 423.

15 See Riordan, J., "Russian fairy tales and their collectors". In Davidson, Hilda E. and Anna Chaudhri (eds) (2003). *A Companion to the Fairy Tale*. Cambridge, Brewer.

began his great Highland collection in 1859.[16] But in England the first in the field was a Cornishman.

The most important early collectors of folktales in Cornwall were Robert Hunt and William Bottrell, both of whom collected in the 1830s, although they published at different dates; it seems too that Hunt drew on some of Bottrell's notes for at least some of his tales.[17] Hunt deserves to be more widely known in both Cornwall and the wider world. In 1829 he embarked upon a ten-month walking tour of Cornwall to collect "every existing tale of the ancient people" though he was not to publish them for another thirty years, In the process, he encountered "droll-tellers", a kind of itinerant minstrel who specialized in long, rambling stories interspersed with songs, which were specifically designed to fit local circumstances.[18] One would love to know more about the storytelling techniques of these men, their repertoire and socio-economic context, but it is clear that their main audience consisted of simple country people. Whether the droll-tellers and the itinerant balladeers were the same people is hard to say.[19] Both Hunt and Bottrell collected stories from non-specialists, ie ordinary working men and women, but also from "gentlemen" and learned "correspondents".

The impetus that drove the collectors was a growing sense that social and technological change were destroying ancient ways of life, and that, while this transformation may have been inevitable and even desirable, it was also important to record the old ways before they were lost forever. The inevitability of the loss was widely accepted, and no real attempt was made to make the old beliefs relevant to the modern age, as Pugin, Morris and the leaders of the

---

16 Howells, William (1831). *Cambrian Superstitions*. London, Longman; (1991) reprint, Felinfach, Llanerch Press. Campbell, J F (1860–61). *Popular Tales of the West Highlands*, 3 vols. Edinburgh, Edmonston and Douglas; (1983–84) reprint, Hounslow, Wildwood House.

17 Harte, Jeremy (2004). *Explore Fairy Traditions*. Loughborough, Heart of Albion.

18 Dorson, Richard M. (1968). *The British Folklorists: A History*. London, Routledge and Kegan Paul, p. 323.

19 Alan Kent thinks not. See Kent, Alan M, (2000). *The Literature of Cornwall: Continuity, Identity, Difference, 1000–2000*. Bristol, Redcliffe Press. But their roles may have overlapped to some extent.

Oxford Movement had all attempted in their different ways.[20] Collectors were therefore ambivalent from the outset; in the main, they were educated men, trained in the dominant culture, who felt a need to distance themselves from the superstitious beliefs of the subject races to which they themselves belonged, even as they recorded them. Some, like Howells in his *Cambrian Superstitions*, were frankly contemptuous:

> We rejoice that the beatific rays of wisdom have gleamed through the dark clouds of ignorance and superstition and the march of intellect has made its appearance even amongst the mountains and valleys of Wales. Almost every peasant can now read, and no longer dreads passing over his threshold in the dark, for fear of coming into contact with "the shadowy shapes of the world unknown".[21]

This unpleasant combination of smugness and self-hatred reflected the ambivalence of the age, and it became less common as the century wore on. Collectors who identified closely with their material would sometimes adopt an apologetic tone. Patrick Kennedy, for instance, apologized for his "legendary fictions", which were "artless in structure, improbable in circumstance, and apparently devoid of purpose",[22] But Kennedy was clear as to his own purpose. His collection was inspired by "the horrid thought that the memory of the tales heard in boyhood would be irrecoverably lost".[23] The Cornish collectors, who had less internalized self-hatred to manage than the Irishman, were less apologetic, but driven by similar motives:

---

20 See Faber, Geoffrey C. (1933). *Oxford Apostles: A Character Study of the Oxford Movement*. London, Faber and Faber; (1954) reprint, Harmondsworth, Penguin Books.

21 Howells, William, *op. cit.* pp. 7–8.

22 Kennedy, Patrick (1891). *Legendary Fictions of the Irish Celts*, 2nd ed. London, Macmillan; (1998) reprint, Felinfach, Llanerch Press.

23 Kennedy, Patrick, *op. cit..* p ix.

In a very few years these interesting traditions would have been lost, unless they had been preserved in some such form as the present volume is intended to supply; since modern customs, and the diffusion of the local news of the day, are superseding, in even the most remote districts, the semi-professional droll-tellers…[24]

In a paradox that often characterized responses to the Victorian transformation, the modern science of folklore collection was used to preserve what remained of the old. Similarly, at Newlyn Stanhope Forbes used the new "plein-air technique", developed in France, to record the passing lifestyles of the Cornish fishing communities.[25]

Both Hunt and Bottrell make the important point that Cornwall, and particularly West Penwith, had until recently been protected from the forces of transformation by its geographical isolation, but that improved transport and communications now made its culture vulnerable to outside influences.

Over the course of the century, folklore acquired academic respectability, and with it a more objective, confident tone. Of course, for all the Celtic collectors, language loss was the elephant in the room. Both Scottish and Manx Gaelic were in decline, though Sophie Morrison's little Manx collection, first published in 1911, is a model of its kind.[26] Welsh was losing its ground, especially in the industrializing south, and Cornish was effectively extinct as a communal language by the time Hunt began collecting.[27] In Ireland, the famine had a disproportionate effect on Irish-speaking

---

24 Bottrell, William (1870). *Traditions and Hearthside Stories of West Cornwall*, 1st series, Penzance; (1996) reprint, Lampeter, Llanerch Press, p v.

25 For instance, his "A Fish Sale on a Cornish Beach", exhibited at the Royal Academy in 1855, and now in the Plymouth City Museums and Art Gallery Collection. See also Birch, Lionel (1906). *Stanhope, A, Forbes A R A, and Elizabeth Stanhope Forbes, A R W S*. London, Cassell.

26 Morrison, Sophia (1911). *Manx Fairy Tales*. London, David Nutt; (1929) reprint, 2nd edn. Douglas Manx Museum and National Trust.

27 Murdoch, Brian (1993). *Cornish Literature*, Cambridge, D S Brewer, especially Chapter 6. "The endurance of the traditional Cornish has been exaggerated by enthusiasts". See, for instance, Berresford Ellis, P (1974). *The Cornish Language*

communities, and Curtin lamented that "no language has been treated with such cruelty and insult by its enemies, and with such treasonable indifference by the majority of the people to whom it belongs as the Gaelic".[28]

Scholarly opinion has been divided about the precise effects of language loss on the storytelling tradition,[29] but there can be little doubt that, in all the Celtic lands, very much has been lost, in both qualitative and quantitative terms. Almost no folklore survives in the Cornish language, and in recording the fragments that do, Morton Nance comments that:

In leaving its own Celtic language and taking to English, Cornwall made a break with tradition that must inevitably have meant the loss of much of the older Cornish folklore.[30]

In the Darwinian struggle to survive that was nineteenth century British capitalism, folkways must have seemed increasingly irrelevant, improbable and destitute of purpose. Urbanization and emigration must also have been responsible for the loss of many stories. The collectors lament what has been lost even as they gather the surviving fragments, and Hunt regretted that the railways "have robbed the west of England of half its interest by dispelling the spectres of romance which were, in hoar antiquity, the ruling spirits of the place"[31] though some folk beliefs even survived the trans-atlantic crossing, and "knockers", the Cornish mine spirits, were heard in Grass Valley, California, as late as the 1930s.[32] The sense

and its Literature. London, Routledge and Kegan Paul, Chapter 5: "The Death of Language".

28 Curtin, Jeremiah (1890). Myths and Folklore of Ireland. London, Sampson, Low, Marston, Searle and Rivington; (1975) reprint, New York, Gramercy, p. 10.

29 Zimmermann, Georges D. (2001). The Irish Storyteller. Dublin, Four Courts Press.

30 Nance, Robert Morton (1924). Folk-lore Recorded in the Cornish Language. 91st Annual Report of the Royal Cornwall Polytechnic Society; (2000) reprint, Penzance, Oakmagic.

31 See Hunt, Robert, op. cit., Introduction.

32 James, Ronald M. (1992). "Knockers, knackers and ghosts. Immigrant folklore in the western mines". In Western Folklore, vol 51, Part 2, 153–177.

of loss that permeated Victorian society was experienced in different senses in the Celtic regions of Britain, which were simultaneously aware of the rapid erosion of ancient cultural paradigms, particularly language and traditional narratives.

Pixies and the people

Apart from the famous giants, Cornwall's most well known contribution to folklore is the Pisgie or Pixie, whose representation is still to be found in a thousand souvenir shops from the Tamar to Land's End. The fairies of tourist art are usually benign, if mischievous-looking figures, rather than, say, the disturbing visions of Victorian painters such as John Anster Fitzgerald and Richard Dadd.[33] But let us look at the stories themselves.

Though we will consider the nature of pixies later, for now we will accept Jacqueline Simpson and Steve Roud's definition of the word "pixy, pisky" as the standard term in Devon, Cornwall and Somerset for a fairy, though many writers from the early nineteenth century onwards have insisted that the two races are quite distinct.[34] Pixies are nowadays associated almost exclusively with Cornwall, but it was on Dartmoor that they encountered their first chronicler, Mrs Anna Eliza Bray, whose letters to her friend the poet Robert Southey were published in 1844 under the title *Legends, Superstitions and Sketches of Devonshire on the Borders of the Tamar and the Tavy*.[35] In fact, Mrs Bray did not have much to say about pixies, though she does give an interesting version of "The midwife to the fairies" (motif F235.4.1, "Fairies made visible through use of ointment"). The belief that fairy mothers required human midwives was widespread, and Deane and Shaw give a Cornish variant (the stories which follow are in my paraphrase):

---

33 Zaczek, Iain (2005). *Fairy Art: Artists and Inspirations*. London, Starfire Publishing.

34 Simpson, Jacqueline and Steve Roud (2000). *A Dictionary of English Folklore*. Oxford, Oxford University Press.

35 Bray, Anna Eliza (1844). *Legends, Superstitions, and Sketches of Devonshire on the Borders of the Tamar and the Tavy*, 2 vols. London, John Murray.

An old midwife was sitting by the fire when there came a knock at the door. She opened it, to see a tiny man sitting on a horse, who told her that his wife was in labour, and in need of help. The old lady mounted the horse behind him, and they rode away to the pisgie's house, where the midwife delivered a child. As she was washing the baby she accidentally wiped some of the soap in her own eye, and found that she could see fairyland all around her. She said nothing, and was escorted home by the grateful father. Some time later, at the local fair she saw the pisgie and greeted him. "With which eye do you see me?" he said. "With the right", she said, pointing to the eye which had been splashed with soap. Instantly the pisgie struck her there, and she remained blind in that eye for as long as she lived.[36]

John Rhys gives a Welsh version of this in the first volume of his *Celtic Folklore*, and Katharine Briggs found another, current at Greenhouse Hill in Yorkshire in the 1920s: interestingly, the hill was said locally to have once been mined by Cornishmen.[37] Pisgies have a close, yet ambivalent relationship with human beings, as the midwife story demonstrates. The tale of Anne Jefferies is a good example of this.

Anne Jefferies and the fairies
In the seventeenth century there lived in St Teath a young woman called Anne. When Anne was nineteen years old, she went into service with Mr Moses Pitt and his family. She was an imaginative girl and would often go out after dark looking for the fairies. But they always ran away before she could see them. One day Anne was sitting at her knitting in the garden, when she heard a rustling in the bushes. When she looked up she spied six little men dressed handsomely in green. One of them jumped up on to her lap and

36 Deane, Tony and Tony Shaw (1975). *The Folklore of Cornwall*. London, Batsford; (1975) reprint, Stroud, Tempus, p. 63.
37 Rhys, John (1901). *Celtic Folklore, Vol 1. Welsh and Manx*, 2 vols. Oxford, Clarendon Press; (1980) reprint, London, Wildwood. Briggs, Katharine (1976). *A Dictionary of Fairies*. London, Allen Lane.

began kissing her, then the others joined him. One of them ran his fingers over her eyes, and suddenly Anne was blinded, and felt that she was flying through the air at great speed. When she opened her eyes again, at a word of command from the fairies, she found herself in a beautiful place, surrounded by palaces of gold and silver, trees full of fruit and flowers, and lakes teeming with gold and silver fish, where birds were singing sweetly. Crowds of finely dressed people were to be seen, strolling and dancing, and Anne was surprised to see that these people were of her own height, and that she herself was dressed in the most beautiful clothes.

Her six friends were still with her, but the finest of them was still her favourite, and the pair managed to separate themselves from the others, and take refuge in a beautiful secluded garden, where they passed the time "lovingly", until their jealous friends arrived with an enraged crowd. Anne's lover drew his sword to defend her, but was wounded.

> The fairy who blinded her before placed his hand on her eyes once more, and again all was dark, and she felt she was flying through the air: when she opened her eyes, she was in the garden again, surrounded by the anxious faces of her friends.[38]

Hunt adds a letter concerning Anne which was written by Moses Pitt to the Bishop of Gloucester, who had interested himself in the matter. She seems to have become something of a local celebrity, was celebrated for her healing powers, and was said to be fed by the fairies. Unfortunately, her supposed supernatural dealings led to her being committed to Bodmin Gaol. This story is unusual (though by no means unique), in that it relates to a real person whose life is documented, though it also incorporates traditional material, and it can clearly be read in a number of ways, not perhaps excluding the psychopathological. Like other stories, such as the tale of Cherry of Zennor, it clearly implies the possibility of erotic relations between pisgies and human beings, in popular belief or fantasy. Uniquely,

---

38 Hunt, Robert, *op. cit.*, pp. 127–29.

the fairies were said to have quoted scripture to the illiterate Anne: "Believe not every spirit, but try the spirits whether they are of God", and this is clearly good advice. In a traditional culture tales such as Anne's could have been used to conceal transgressive behaviour or sexual fantasy, especially among lonely servant girls: there are clearly elements of wish-fulfilment in Anne's story, and it may also have raised her status as a practitioner of traditional healing, and so conferred some economic advantage.

II
Changelings

Encounters with the fairy folk could certainly be hazardous, if alluring, and indeed dangerous, especially for newborn babies; as Simpson and Roud explain:

> In societies where the belief in fairies was strong, it was held that they could steal human babies and substitute one of their own race: the latter would never thrive.[39]

These stories are frequently found associated with the Cornish pixies, and Hartland gives other versions in his classic survey, mostly from Wales and Scotland.[40] Simpson and Roud found only one English example, from Kington in Herefordshire, though Westwood and Simpson do rather better in *The Lore of the Land*, with examples from Staffordshire and Suffolk, as well as the Kington case.[41] But there is no doubt that changelings are mostly found in the Celtic lands, where they seem to go back a long way, and were known variously as "Corpán Sidhe" (Irish), "Stodhlbhradh" (Scottish Gaelic) and the Manx "Lhiannoo Shee". In Welsh this is "plentyn an newidwyd amarall", but no Cornish word for changeling seems to have survived.[42]

---

39 Simpson and Roud, *op. cit.*, pp. 53–54.

40 Hartland, Edwin Sidney (1891). *The Science of Fairy Tales: An Inquiry into Fairy Mythology*. London, Walter Scott, Chapters III and IV.

41 Westwood, J. and J. Simpson (2005). *The Lore of the Land*. London, Penguin.

42 See MacKillop, James (1998). *Dictionary of Celtic Mythology*. Oxford, OUP.

One of the best Cornish changeling stories is Bottrell's "The Changeling of Brea Vean" from his 1870 collection: One day in harvest time a woman called Jenny Trayer, who lived at the foot of Carn Brea near Redruth, fed her baby and rocked it to sleep, and then went out to help with the reaping. When she returned, the cradle was overturned and the baby was missing. Then, searching around the cottage she found the child asleep in a corner. But the baby never seemed right to her after that—it was always unhappy and bad tempered, and the more it ate the leaner it became. Neighbours said Jenny had been tricked by the small people, and advised her to bathe the baby in the chapel well, "as May comes around". She tried this twice, without success, then, as she went the third time, Jenny passed some large rocks by the open moor, and heard a shrill voice from above her head, crying:

"Tredrill! Tredrill!
Thy wife and children greet thee well!"

Then the child on her shoulder seemed to reply:

"What care I for wife or child, when I ride on Dowdy's back
to chapel well and have got pap my full?"

The frightened woman ran home and a neighbour advised her to place the child on the ash-heap and beat it. The squire rode by, saw what they were doing and stopped them, but later Jenny left the child under a stile on the church-way path. When she returned home she found her own child asleep on some dry straw, spotlessly clean and wrapped in a piece of old-fashioned chintz, of the kind which fairies love to steal from furze bushes when it is left out to dry. The boy grew up simple, and subject to fits, though he made a good shepherd. He liked to wander by himself in wild places and people said that he spoke with the fairies.[43]

---

43 Bottrell, William, *op. cit.*, pp. 113–18.

Some of these stories could be seen as attempts to rationalize the incidence of infantile congenital illnesses, such as Down's Syndrome, which were little understood at the time. Some could also represent ways of understanding puerperal depression and neglect. Certainly young children were very vulnerable in nineteenth-century Cornwall, and the large-scale emigration of working fathers must have made it more difficult for hard-pressed mothers to cope. Most mining families lived in hovels of cob and thatch, which they often built for themselves. Sanitation and water supplies were poor, smallpox, measles, diphtheria and typhoid fever were rife, and the burial register of St Just in Penwith demonstrates the inevitable results. In the decade 1840−49, 600 males were buried in that town; their average age was twenty-five years and eight months; 201 were infant boys of less than five years. Of the 477 females, 220 were under five years of age. These figures of course also demonstrate the shocking fatality rate among miners,[44] just as they provide evidence for an overwhelming grief which must have been as communal as it was individual.

That the fairy belief itself could be used to rationalize or even motivate child abuse, though it can never have been common, is evident from a small number of documented cases. In the *West Briton* of July 14th, 1843 there appeared the story of a Penzance man called Trevelyan, who was charged with starving and beating his infant son. At Christmas 1841 the child was left out in the cold for hours, because his parents believed him to be a changeling.[45] The case failed for lack of evidence, but the family were driven out of town. It is interesting that, while the parents presumably thought that the changeling hypothesis would excuse their barbarous behaviour, their neighbours did not agree, whether they believed in fairies or not. One imagines that these parents had a variety of problems, some of which were blamed on their unfortunate infant, and on the pixies.

One feels that pixies are also maligned in another story which appeared in the *Western Daily Mercury* on June 6th, 1890: A few days

---

44 Rowe, John (1953). *Cornwall in the Age of the Industrial Revolution*. Liverpool, Liverpool University Press, p. 151.

45 Deane and Shaw, *op. cit.*, p. 64.

previously some labourers were stripping bark in the woods near Torrington. One of the men went back to retrieve a tool. And as he stooped to pick it up he found himself unable to stand up straight again. He heard loud laughter all around, and realized that he had been trapped by the pixies. After remaining like this for five hours, he was eventually able to crawl away on his hands and knees, and eventually got home, when his wife berated him for not turning his pockets inside out (a deterrent against fairy magic).[46]

Of course a man might have many reasons for being late home from work, but the interesting thing about this story is that the man considered being "pixy-led" a reasonable explanation, and that his wife did in fact believe him.

But if pixies were sometimes maligned in this way, they were often given the credit for good deeds too. They seem to have been particularly fond of human children. Deane and Shaw tell the story of the lost child of St Allen:

A small boy was picking flowers one evening in summer when he heard music. He followed it into a wood, and to the side of a lake, where he met a beautiful lady who led him into an underground cave made of crystal. Many days later he was found by his distraught parents asleep in the ferns. He told them his story, which has been told since then in the district of North Trur.[47]

Crossing tells two stories of farmers on Dartmoor whose threshing was done for them by friendly fairies, and also the tale of "The Ploughman's Breakfast": One morning a man was ploughing on one of the moorland farms, and was starting to feel hungry. As he passed a large granite outcrop in the middle of the field he heard a voice crying "The oven's hot!" "Bake me a cake, then!" replied the hungry ploughman, continuing to plough his furrow. When he passed the same spot again he found a freshly baked cake awaiting him on the rock, steaming hot. The man knew that the pixies had taken pity on his hunger, and ate the cake gratefully.[48]

---

46 Crossing, William (1890). *Tales of the Dartmoor Pixies: Glimpses of Elfin Haunts and Antics*. London, Hood, p. 93.

47 Deane and Shaw, *op. cit.*, p. 64.

48 Crossing, *op. cit.*, pp. 71–3.

In general this type of story reinforces values such as reciprocity and diligence, which are esteemed in a small rural community, and which affirm and sustain its existence. But it is also true that people who have had close and lengthy encounters with the fairies seem often to be changed in some profound way, as was Jenny Trayer's son in Hunt's story above. Or poor Cherry of Zennor, who was employed by a fairy "gentleman" to look after his child, seems to have fallen in love with him, but was eventually rejected by him because of her insatiable curiosity.[49] This story, which has some interesting parallels with Apuleius's ancient story "Cupid and Psyche",[50] ends sadly, for Cherry "was never afterward right in her head, and on moonlight nights, until she died, she would wander on to the Lady Downs to look for her master".

This kind of behaviour is of course characteristic of grief. Murray Parkes, in his classic study of bereavement, contended that:

> The searching behaviour of the bereaved person is not "aimless" at all. It has the specific aim of finding the person who is gone. But the bereaved person seldom admits to having so irrational an aim and his behaviour is therefore regarded by others and himself as "aimless". His search for "something to do" is bound to fail, because the things he can do are not, in fact, what he wants to do at all. What he wants is to find the lost person.[51]

Cherry, like Jenny in Hunt's story of "The Fairy Widowers" and perhaps Anne Jefferies, is mourning a lost love, and therefore searching, just as the mothers in the "Changeling" stories are searching for their lost children.

---

49 Hunt, Robert, *op. cit.*, pp. 120–26.
50 Apuleius (1950). *The Golden Ass*. Trans Robert Graves, Harmondsworth, Penguin, Chapters VII–IX.
51 Murray Parkes, C (1972). *Bereavement: Studies of Grief in Adult Life*. London, Tavistock Publications; (1975) reprint, Harmondsworth, Penguin, p. 66.

Pixie origins

We have considered the social and economic background to the great Cornish folklore collections of the nineteenth century, and looked at some of the stories about pixies which were gathered at that time. Scholarly debate has tended to focus on their taxonomy and origins: opinions on how pixies look and behave tend to be unanimous, if sometimes ambiguous.[52] They dress in green, and may be either diminutive in size, like Shakespeare's fairies, or of ordinary human height. They seem, at least sometimes, to occupy a distinct social world of their own, which parallels the human, but has some idealized, perhaps archaic qualities (Hunt has a fairy fair, and even the funeral of a pixy queen)[53] and the stories themselves mostly deal with what happens when the two worlds meet, as in the tales of Anne Jefferies and Cherry of Zennor, above. They are mischievous, and may lead people astray on dark nights, or take babies, leaving their own misshapen offspring in exchange, though they may also be kind to children or to people they like or pity, as in Crossing's "Ploughman" story. Crossing also tells us that: "in many an ancient farmhouse [we] shall be told how the butter has been made, and the corn in the barn has been threshed by these industrious little goblins".[54]

Like human beings, pixies may be kind or cruel, creative or destructive. Also they are fickle, and their favour can be easily lost, as in the widespread story of "The Fairy Ointment", in which an inquisitive human is punished for inquisitiveness; and in Bottrell's "The Fairy Master", for instance.[55] In fact, relationships between human beings and fairies seem to have been very ambivalent.

On the basis of his researches, Hunt identified five clearly distinguishable varieties of the Cornish fairy family, namely:[56]

---

52 Hunt, Robert, *op. cit.*, pp. 115−18.

53 Hunt, Robert, *op. cit.*, pp. 102−03.

54 Crossing, *op. cit.*, p. 2.

55 Bottrell, William, *op. cit.*, pp. 92−103.

56 Hunt, Robert, *op. cit.*, p. 80.

1. The Small People
2. The Spriggans
3. Piskeys or Pisgeys
4. Buccas, Bockles or Knockers
5. The Brownies

It seems that this classification has more to do with function than with essential difference: spriggans, for instance, seem to function as bodyguards specifically, and knockers and buccas work in the mines.[57] In common usage too, these different terms may well have lacked precision. In her exhaustive categorization, Katharine Briggs classified pixies with other tutelary spirits, such as brownies and Irish "pooka" (i.e., *púca*),[58] but Diana Purkiss, while admiring Briggs's "vast and entertaining taxonomies", considers them too fragmented: in her view there are only four fairy types, namely:[59]

1. Brownies, Hobs
2. Fairy guides
3. Fairy societies
4. Poltergeists and tricksters

---

57 Unlike many of their relatives, knockers seem to have survived the transatlantic crossing, and are recorded in California (as 'tommyknockers') as late as the 1930s. See James (1992), pp. 153–77. They survive to this day in a common American nursery rhyme:

> 'Late last night and the night before,
> Tommyknockers, Tommyknockers,
> Knocking at the door.
> I want to go out, don't know if I can,
> Because I'm so afraid
> Of the Tommyknocker man.'

The rhyme in turn inspired Stephen King's *The Tommyknockers* (1988). London, Hodder and Stoughton. This lively horror novel is set in New England and contains nothing which is authentically western, let alone Cornish, but it is an interesting example of how folk beliefs can travel and morph in unexpected ways.

58 Briggs, Katherine (1967). *The Fairies in Tradition and Literature*. London, Routledge, pp. 28–30.

59 Purkiss, Diane (2000). *Troublesome Things: A History of Fairies and Fairy Stories*. London, Allen Lane; (2007) reprinted as *Fairies and Fairy Stories: A History*. London, Tempus Publishing.

Brownies are small, shaggy men, often dressed in rags, who perform household tasks and help around the farm: they flourish mainly in Scotland and all over the north and east of England. Some Cornish pixies do seem to perform this role, though it is not their dominant characteristic. They often do live in societies of a sophisticated kind, and they are certainly tricksters. Deane and Shaw identify only three types of Cornish fairy: knockers, piskeys and spriggans,[60] and opinions will no doubt continue to differ: pixies are liminal and protean, and will continue to defy our attempts to contain and classify them.

In the past, much energy has also gone into debating the origin of pixies. It was often said that they were the souls of Cornwall's prehistoric inhabitants, supposed to be getting smaller and smaller with the years, until they eventually vanish. Thus "the dwindling of the pixies would represent their loss of power, and account for their eagerness to get hold of human changelings to reinforce their weakening stock".[61]

This would agree with similar beliefs in comparable cultures, such as the Irish, and Briggs adds that: "The Christian theory that the fairies are fallen angels seems to be the next in popularity", a belief which is also found in Ireland. The knockers were said to be the spirits of deceased Jews who had been put to work in the mines as a punishment for their alleged role in the crucifixion of Christ. The idea that pixies are memories or actual survivors of some earlier, prehistoric race has proved surprisingly durable, but seems to be a romantic delusion, perhaps based on a semantic confusion between "peck", a Scottish word for goblin, "Pict" referring to the ancient inhabitants of the British Isles, and the Cornish pisgie or pixie. In fact picti means "painted ones" and was Roman army slang: no-one knows what the Picts called themselves. Yet even Henry Jenner, the great Cornish language scholar, concluded that:

> The Cornish piskie is a mixed conception, founded partly
> on a folk-memory, or perhaps even more than a folk memory
> of a small, dark savage pre-Celtic race which certainly once

60 Deane and Shaw, *op. cit.*

61 Briggs, Katherine, *op. cit.*, p. 143.

existed and may have continued down to comparatively recent times. …The pre-Celtic small people who were for some reason or other called "picti", though not necessarily as the Picts of Roman British and early English and Scottish history, and the Cornish-speaking Celts of the Dumnonian kingdom, followed the usual rule of their language and make "pict" into "pix", whence came "pixy" and "pisky"[62]

though he offers no evidence to support this hypothesis.

Katherine Briggs concluded that pixies represent the spirits of the dead:

At first sight the commonly received idea of fairy land seems as far as possible from the shadowy and bloodless realms of the dead, and yet, in studying fairy lore and ghost lore alike we are haunted and teased by resemblances between them. … Some classes of the dead were undoubtedly regarded by the old people as inhabitants of fairyland.[63]

And even the recently deceased might find themselves among the pixies, as in Bottrell's interesting story "The Fairy Dwelling on Selena Moor", in which a man called William Noy meets his dead sweetheart Grace Hutchens, in an assembly of moorland fairies: "Grace assured Mr Noy of her everlasting love, …and also told him that when he died, if he wished to join her, they would than be united and dwell in this fairy land of the moors."[64]

Of all these different theories, Briggs' is the most convincing, but it is interesting that, despite their differences, all of these hypotheses explain pixies in terms of the past, in terms of some individual or communal loss. Fairyland is the abode of dead races, lost cultures, babies and sweethearts.

---

62 Jenner, Henry (1916). "Piskies: a folk-lore study". In Jones, K I (ed) (1996). *Cornish Fairy Folk*. Penzance, Oakmagic, pp. 24−5.

63 Briggs, Katherine (1979). "The fairies and the realm of the dead". In *Folklore*, vol 81, pp. 81−96.

64 Bottrell, William, *op. cit.*, pp. 32−40.

Conclusion

In terms of both content and context therefore, these stories are permeated with a sense of loss. As far back as the seventeenth century John Aubrey could lament that:

> Now-a-days bookes are common, and most of the poor people understand letters; and the many good Bookes, and variety of Turnes of Affaires, have putt all the old Fables out of doors, and the divine art of Printing and Gunpowder, have frighted away Robin Goodfellow and the Fayries.[65]

It may be that the whole folklore project was always driven by this sense of loss, but there can be little doubt that this was sharpened in nineteenth century Britain by the Industrial Revolution and the many changes which came in its wake.

The cultural response to change was of course ambivalent. An age of bourgeois liberalism and (hesitant) democratic progress tended to see the past as barbarous, autocratic and superstitious. This tendency was dramatized in gothic fiction, such as Mrs Radcliffe's *The Mysteries of Udolpho*, and Matthew Lewis' *The Monk*.[66] The tension between progress and optimism on the one hand, and loss and pessimism on the other, tended to deepen as the century wore on and the true costs of industrialization became apparent. This is why, although the first publishers of folktales were apologetic about their collections, the later ones were not. And thus, in his preface to the play *Gwreans an Bys* (*The Creation of the World, A Cornish Mystery*) in 1826, Davies Gilbert could write:

> No-one more sincerely rejoices, than does the Editor of this ancient mystery, that the Cornish ... language has ceased altogether from being used by the inhabitants of Cornwall.[67]

---

65 Dorson, *op. cit.*, p. 6.

66 See also Punter, David (1980). *The Literature of Terror*. London, Longman; and Baldick, Chris (ed) (1992). *The Oxford Book of Gothic Tales*. Oxford, Oxford University Press.

67 The play appears in a number of anthologies. See, for example, *Gwreans an Bys. The Creation of the World, A Cornish Mystery* (1864). Translated and edited by

Yet fifty years later Henry Jenner was to read his paper on "The Cornish Language" to the Philological Society, and the language revival began to take off around the turn of the century.[68] As we have seen, this sense that valuable things were being swept away, and needed to be preserved, also informed the folklore collectors, and perhaps generated a new audience for their work. Dorson captures this sense of loss in his description of Hunt's work, (see Introduction).

Of course, large swathes of rural Britain remained relatively untouched by industrialization, though improved communications, agricultural depression, and a phenomenal rate of urban growth would affect most people's lives, but the transformation was particularly evident in Cornwall where, as Philip Payton has noted, "the economy was one of the very first in the world to industrialise".[69] Investment in tin and copper transformed the Cornish way of life and landscape, and by 1824 the parish of Gwennap alone was responsible for more than a third of global production of copper ore, while mining in Cornwall was technologically the most advanced in the world. Cornish engines and engineers were exported to the furthest corners of the globe.[70] This resulted in what Alan Kent has called "an outstanding vision of industrial confidence and revived identity",[71] though it must have been challenging to live through. In any case, renewed confidence gave way to despair in "the Hungry Forties", when the rigidity and overspecialization of the Cornish economy began to be exposed. The result was starvation, com-pounded by the failure of the potato crop, as in Scotland and Ireland, emigration on a huge scale, and violent riots, in Helston, Penzance and elsewhere.[72] Prices rose steeply, and mine work continued to be difficult and dangerous—it has been estimated that in 1847 one in

---

Whitley Stokes for the Philological Society, London, Williams and Norgate.

68 See Williams, Derek R. (ed) (2004). *Henry and Katharine Jenner: A Celebration of Cornwall's Culture, Language and Identity*. London, Francis Boutle.

69 Payton, Philip (1996). *Cornwall*. Fowey, Alexander Associates. Revised edition (2004). *Cornwall: A History*. Fowey, Cornwall Editions, p. 180 *et seq.*

70 Rolt, L. T. C. (1970). *Victorian Engineering*. London, Allen Lane, pp. 59–67.

71 Kent, Alan M.. *The literature of Cornwall*. Bristol: Radcliffe.

72 Payton, Philip, *op. cit.*

every five miners in Gwennap died or were disabled in accidents.[73] Whole communities were decimated by emigration, as we have seen.

And the communities which were most disrupted by these catastrophic events were the same communities from which Hunt and Bottrell gathered their drolls. At the same time, the cultural annexation of Cornwall proceeded apace, as the isolation which had protected the far west for so long was eroded by improved transport and communications. Though it was still possible for Wilkie Collins to "ramble beyond railways" in 1850, the Duchy was increasingly being incorporated into the British state.[74] Most of the people who survived (or did not survive) these events have left no record of their thoughts and feelings, and social change on this scale was quite unprecedented, and must have generated huge stresses, on both individual and communal levels. We thus have a profound experience of loss occurring simultaneously in a number of interconnected domains—the British, the Cornish, the communal, the familial and individual, and it was from this background that the pixie stories emerged and found their audience.

Of course, people have always told and listened to stories, for entertainment and to help them make sense of the world.

> Through the centuries (if not millennia) during which, in their retelling, fairy tales became ever more refined, they came to convey at the same time overt and covert meanings—came to speak simultaneously to all levels of the human personality, communicating in a manner which reaches the uneducated mind of the child as well as that of the sophisticated adult.[75]

---

73 Halliday, F. E. (19590. *A History of Cornwall*. London Gerald Duckworth, p. 291.

74 Collins, Wilkie (1851). *Rambles Beyond Railways*. London, Richard Bentley; (1982) reprint, London, A Mott.

75 Bettelheim, Bruno (1976). *The Uses of Enchantment: The Meaning and Importance of Fairy Tales*. New York, Alfred A Knopt; (1978) reprint, Harmondsworth, Penguin, p. 4.

The stories collected in Cornwall seem more directed at adults, from Hunt's account, though children must have heard them often. And what is the major theme of the stories but loss—lost children, lost lovers, lost races? And the accommodation of loss is an internal, as well as an external process, which narrative can address simultaneously. As Brian Wicker reminds us:

> ... narrative is not only a unique instrument for describing certain kinds of truth about the external world, it is also, for similar reasons, uniquely important in explaining what happens inside oneself.[76]

The Cornish working class community experienced all kinds of loss and change, emigration, and workplace fatalities, on top of the customary high mortality rates of the time, especially in relation to children and childbirth: it is striking how many pixie stories contain the "midwife" motif or deal with the loss of children, such as "The lost child of St Allen". In addition, industrial, economic and cultural changes, such as language loss, must have impinged upon individual and communal identities, and to such losses communal answers must be found so that continuity and meaning can be recovered.[77] It may be that one such communal response to loss was to gather together to tell and listen to stories, or rather, that an ancient, dying tradition acquired temporary importance by providing an outlet for grief and an opportunity to share it. And in passing the stories on to Hunt and Bottrell, the people shared their loss and the healing power of their stories with a wider audience which was itself struggling to manage change.

Though we do not know as much about storytelling in nineteenth-century Cornwall as we would like, it is evident (from the better documented Irish tradition, for instance), that the communal setting allowed emotional responses to be shared, in ways which would inhibit the development of pathological grief, Freud's "melancholia",

---

76 Wicker, Brian (1975). *The Story Shaped World: Fiction and Metaphysics*. London, Athlone Press, p. 46.

77 Marris, Peter (1974). *"Loss and change". Reports of The Institute of Community Studies*. London, Routledge and Kegan Paul.

or what we would describe as depression.[78] The point (or at least one point) of the pixie stories was to help people cope with loss and change, not least by affirming the continued viability of the community in coming together to share these stories, and so to share and heal their pain.

---

78 Freud, Sigmund (1917). "Mourning and melancholia". In Strachey, James (ed). *The Standard Edition of the Complete Psychological Works of Sigmund Freud.* London, Hogarth Press, Vol 14, pp. 239–60. (Translation of "Trauer und Melancholie", *Internationale Zeitschrift für Psychoanalyse*, Vol 4, No 6, 288–301.)

Chapter 2

The Giant and the Knocker

I

The Stories

In the British Isles, as elsewhere, stories about giants are mostly found in the Highland zone, to the north and west. So we find, for instance, the Fomorians of Tory Island, Ysbaddaden Bencaur in the story of "Culhwch and Olwen", and the adventures of Cuchullain among the Scottish giants.[1] In southern Britain, Cornwall has always stood out for its number of giant tales, and within Cornwall itself they are often associated with the far west. Often they are depicted as the creators of landscape, features which appear to be artificial yet are beyond the strength of ordinary men,[2] and this is why the Cornish countryside is dotted with names like the Giant's Cave at Lemorna, the Giant's Hand on Carn Brea, and the Giant's Hedge at Looe.[3] Giant's "Quoits" are particularly common, as at Lanyon, Trevethy and elsewhere, for instance.[4] The context of the stories thus places the giant firmly in the context of myth of origin, and in

---

1   See MacKillop, James (1998). *Dictionary of Celtic Mythology*. Oxford, Oxford University Press, pp. 211–12. Spence, Lewis (1948). *The Minor Traditions of British Mythology*. London, Rider and Co, pp. 71–86. Jones, Gwyn and Jones, Thomas (1949). *The Mabinogion*. London, J M Dent, pp. 95–136.

2   Westwood, Jennifer and Simpson, Jacqueline (2005). *The Lore of the Land: A Guide to England's Legends, from Spring-Heeled Jack to the Witches of Warboys*. London, Penguin, p. 628.

3   Hunt, Robert (1881). *Popular Romances of the West of England* (3rd edition). London, Chatto and Windus, p. 43.

4   Deane, Tony and Shaw, Tony (2003). *Folklore of Cornwall*. Stroud, Tempus Publishing, pp. 66–7. These are often the capstones of ancient tombs. Surprisingly, the Cornish language has no word for 'quoit'.

the past giants were often seen as a memory of ancient gods.[5] However, this may be, there is no doubt that giants are firmly embedded in the Cornish landscape. For instance, the giants of Trecrobben, commonly named Trencrom, a rough granite hill near Llant to the west of Carn Brea, built a castle whose four entrances "still remain in Cyclopean massiveness" to attest the Herculean powers by which such mighty blocks were piled upon each other, and there the giants conducted human sacrifice. Their gold and jewels were hidden in the caves, "in the days of their troubles, when they were perishing before the conquerors of their land". Their treasures remain to this day, guarded by spriggans.[6] Interestingly, Hunt sets this ancient legend carefully in the new industrial landscape of his own time where:

> … around the towns of Cambourne and Redruth are seen
> hundreds of miners' cottages, and scores of tall chimneys
> telling of the mechanical appliances which are brought to
> bear upon the extraction of tin and copper from the earth.[7]

Though the old treasures of the giants may be kept safe by the spriggans, who are considered by some to be the ghosts of the giants, modern man has power to make the earth give up its ancient mineral wealth.[8]

The associations with stone, buried treasure, and human sacrifice or cannibalism are characteristic of the giant and his stories. Stupidity is also a common feature, as in Hunt's story of the giant Bolster.

---

5   See for instance Spence, Lewis (1937). *Legendary London: Early London in Tradition and History*. London, Robert Hale and Co, pp. 151–52.

6   Hunt, Robert *op. cit.*, p. 51.

7   Hunt, Robert *op. cit.*, pp. 49–50.

8   Deane and Shaw, *op. cit.*, p. 65. Spriggans are warrior fairies who can alter their size at will. They are often associated with cromlechs, ancient barrows and buried treasure.

Bolster lived on the hill once known as Carne Bury-anacht, the sparstone grave now called St Agnes' beacon, He was such an immense size that he could stand with one foot on the beacon and the other on Carn Brea six miles away, as shown in Cruikshank's striking frontispiece to Hunt's book. Bolster had a wife, and he made her work clearing stones. He fell in love with the beautiful Saint Agnes, who would not reciprocate, and who grew tired of him pestering her. Eventually she asked him to prove his love for her by filling a hole in the cliff at Chapel Porth with his blood. Bolster thought he could do this with ease, and cut his arm to allow the blood to flow. Hour after hour it flowed, but still the hole was not filled because, as the saint had known all along, the hole opened out into the sea, and so the giant died, and the hole at Chapel Porth is stained red to this day.[9]

Apart from being stupid and gullible, giants were often malevolent, cannibalistic ogres, though by the time these stories were collected they seem often to have degenerated into figures of fun, and, though they emerge from a dark, primeval past they inhabit a recognizably nineteenth-century world peopled by tinkers, cobblers and fishermen.[10] Nonetheless, giants were the aboriginal inhabitants of the land. In legendary history, Brutus, leader of the Trojans who invaded and named Britain, sent his deputy Corineus to govern Cornwall, because "it was there the giants were most numerous".[11] Giants tend not to be individualized, and are usually anonymous, with the exception of the oddly-named Bolster, "John of Gaunt, Jack of the Giant's Hedge, Wrath of Ralph's Cupboard and Dan Dynas of Teryn Dinas". As to their personal appearance:

> … what giants looked like can be pieced out from various stories. The great earthworks they lived in seemed naturally

---

9   Hunt, Robert, *op. cit.*, pp. 73–75. My paraphrase, as elsewhere.

10 Briggs, Katherine (1967). *The Fairies in English Tradition and Literature*. London, Bellew Publishing, pp. 62–63.

11 See *Geoffrey of Monmouth: Historia Regum Britannia*, ed Acton Griscom (1929). New York.

the work of huge men. So they ranged in height from Bolster, who could strike a double league, down to Tom of Bowyeyheer in Ludguan. And he was a mere eight foot. They are said to have dwindled in size from generation to generation, like the fairies.[12]

Though often bowdlerized for a child audience, the stories show that giants were dangerous. The Nancledry giant "lived principally on little children, whom he is said to have swallowed whole", and the Tribiggan giant lived on children which he fried on a flat rock. They could be sexually predatory too, as we have seen in the case of Bolster and Saint Agnes; at Treryn one giant killed another, and took his wife.[13] These behaviours, combined with their associations with caves and "castles" suggest an identification with the Freudian Id, "das Es":[14]

… the instinctual pole of the personality; its contents, as an expression of the instincts, are unconscious, a portion of them being hereditary and innate, a portion repressed and acquired.[15]

And in one particularly moving story a foolish but good-natured giant commits murder unconsciously, almost out of love:

---

12 Westwood and Simpson, *op. cit.*, p. 628. But 'Dan Dynas' just means 'Den an Dynas', 'the man of the castle'.

13 Spooner, Barbara (1965). "The Giants of Cornwall" *Folklore*, v76, 1, pp. 16–32.

14 These associations are equally strong in Manx folklore. Castle Rushden has an enchanted chamber which was inhabited by fairies, then by giants until Merlin bound them in spells. People who tried to explore the underground caverns in which they lived would mysteriously disappear. Subterranean passages are said to lead to a beautiful land of giants, and there are also memories of a three-headed Danish giant buried on top of the Karrin. See Moore, A W (1891). *The Folklore of the Isle of Man.* Reprinted Llanerch (1991).

15 Laplanch, Jean and Pontalis, Jean-Bertrand (1988). *The Language of Psychoanalysis.* London, Karnac Books, and the Institute of Psychoanalysis, p. 197.

The giant of Carn Galva was a gentle character who protected the people from the more warlike giants of Lelant. He was a playful, sociable giant, fond of a young fellow from Choone, who used to visit him. One day they were playing Quoits, when the giant "tapped" his playfellow on the head with the tips of his fingers. At the same time he said, "be sure to come again tomorrow, my son, and we will have a capital game of bob."

But the giant's fingers had gone right through the boy's skull, and though he tried to save him it was no use. The giant mourned for his dead friend, but in seven years or so he pined away and died of a broken heart. The logan stone on which he used to rock himself remains at Zennor.[16]

Tom and the Tinkeard

The most ambitious giant story is the story of Tom and the Tinkeard, a "droll" and therefore part of the professional story-teller's repertoire, which is told by both Hunt and Bottrell. Here is a summary of Hunt's version:

A lad named Tom once lived in Lelant. Though rather lazy, he was very strong, and didn't appear so very big in those days, when all men were twice the size they are now. Tom finally got a job drawing a brewer's dray, and on the road to St Ives he came across a score of men trying to move a fallen tree. Tom got down and lifted the tree unaided. A little further on the road bent to bypass a giant's house. Tom carried on to St Ives, but on his way back he decided to take a short cut through the giant's gate. After a while he came to the giant's castle and the giant ran out, shouting angrily, "What business have you here?" Tom defied him, and the giant tore up a tree and charged him.

Tom tore out the wheel and axle from his cart and prepared to defend himself. Blunderbuss the giant slipped

16 Bottrell, William (1880). *Stories and Folklore of West Cornwall*, third series. Reprinted Llanerch (1996), pp. 122–23.

THE GIANT AND THE KNOCKERS

and was impaled on Tom's axle. Tom tried in vain to save the giant's life, and in gratitude Blunderbuss left him his wealth, his livestock and land, saying "take them all, only bury me decent". Tom fixed his cart and drove back to Marazion, where he resigned his job at the brewery, Then he and his wife, Jane, went back to bury the giant and take possession of his castle.

The next episode of the droll entitled "Tom, the giant, his wife Jane, and Jack the Tinkeard", was, Hunt tells us, often performed as a "geese dance" at Christmastide, a kind of fancy dress dance involving cross-dressing which was apparently unique to west Cornwall. It introduces a new character, a "tinkeard" or tinker who:

> … wore such a coat as was never seen in the West Country before. It was made of a shaggy bull's hide, dressed whole with the hair on. The skin of the forelegs made the sleeves, the hindquarters only were cut, pieces being let in to make the spread of the skits, while the neck and skin of the head formed a sort of head. The whole appeared as hard as iron, and when Tom fought the Tinkeard it sounded as if the coat roared like thunder. The two fought and Tom got the worst of it, until eventually he cried, "I believe thou art the devil, and no man. Let's see they feet before thou dost taste any more of my blood". But the tinkeard showed Tom he had no cloven foot.[17]

Tom took the tinkeard home, they became good friends and, as Hunt says, "the story ordinarily rambles on". The tinkeard describes his journey from his distant home across the land of Cornwall:

> In this land there were many giants, who digged for tin and other treasures. With these giants he had lived and worked— they always treated him well. Indeed, he always found the bigger the man the more gentle. Half the evil that's told

17 Hunt, Robert, *op. cit.*, p. 61.

about them by cowardly folks who fear to go near them is false.[18]

The tinkeard never knew father or mother, or had a home to call his own, but had been christened Jack by a travelling tin merchant who took a fancy to him. Jack taught Tom how to plough, and plant a vegetable garden, the first in Cornwall, and showed his wife Jane how to brew beer. He also showed Tom how to slaughter and skin beasts. Various adventures ensue, and eventually Tom and Jane fall out. Jane goes back to her mother and gives birth to a son called Honey, who is suckled by a goat.

In another important episode, Tom accidentally uncovers a heap of black and grey stones by the castle wall, while playing Quoits. "By the gods!" exclaims Jack, "It's all the richest tin!" Tom had never heard of tin, so Jack showed him how to dress it. Later Jack and Jane find a secret room in the castle, containing the bones of the old giant's wives, along with a hoard of splendid clothes and jewels.

The episodic narrative continues, and includes the defeat of the Lord of Pengerswick, an enchanter who tries to steal the secret of the tin, but is thwarted by Jack. Jack then felt a longing to go back to his distant home on Dartmoor, where he found the giant Dart on his deathbed, and forced him to give up his wealth. Having buried the giant and settled his mother's affairs, he returned to Cornwall, where he married Tom's daughter. But first Tom asked him to dispose of a troublesome giant who lived in Morva. Tom and Jack threw quoits at the giant's house, and when he came out and chased them down the hill he fell into a trap which Jack had prepared in advance. Jack married Tom's daughter, and young Tom married a Morva girl.[19] At the joint wedding there was a great feast, with wrestling, hurling and quoits.

For all its episodic liveliness, the "Tom and the Tinkeard" saga enacts the origins of a community. Aspects of it are archaic—Jack's strange coat, for instance, and Tom and his wheel and axle recalls images of the ancient Celtic sky gods.[20] Such images take us back to

---

18 Hunt, Robert, *op. cit.*, p. 63.

19 For all the above, see Hunt, Robert, *op. cit.*, pp. 55−72.

20 See Green, Miranda (1986). *The Gods of the Celts.* pp. 39−72. And for the

the dawn of European thought; Jack in his hide coat even recalls the "sorcerers" depicted in the caves of Les Trois Frères.[21] (The discovery and publication of Palaeolithic art accelerated rapidly throughout the nineteenth century, and peaked in the early decades of the twentieth.) The stories also explain and celebrate some of the key elements of Cornishness, wrestling and tin, agriculture and mining, coming to an end in a communal enactment stretching far into the future, as Margaret Courtney wrote in 1886:

> On the following Monday (ie after August 1st) there was formerly a large fair, and though Morvah is a very small village without any attractions, the farmers flocked to it in great numbers to drink and feast, sitting on the hedges of the small fields common in west Cornwall, "Three on one horse, like going to Morvah Fair", is an old proverb.[22] Jack's discovery and sale of tin was also celebrated at Marazion.[23]

II
Folklore and Social Change

Robert Hunt foregrounds giants under the section devoted to "Romances and Superstitions of the Mythic Ages", the time when conceptions of the Aryan gods first arose,[24] though Hunt of course does not attribute divinity to the giants, at the beginning of his *Popular Romances of the West of England*, first published in 1865, and fronted by Cruikshank's wonderful illustration of "the giant Bolster striding

archaisms of the story generally, McMahon, Brendan (1996). "The Cornish giant myth", In *An Baner Kernewek*, 85, August 1996.

21 Breait, H. (1952). *400 Centuries of Cave Art Montignac*. Centre d'Etudes et de Documentation Pre Historiques.

22 See Gimbutas, Marija (1989). *The Language of the Goddess*. London, Thames and Hudson. Chapter 17: "Male gods and daimones", pp. 175−186. Also Laming, Manette (1959). *Lascoux. Paintings and Engravings*. Harmondsworth, Penguin.

23 Courtney, Margaret (1886). *Cornish Feasts and Folklore*. Reprinted Oakmagic (1998).

24 See Müller, Max (1909). *Comparative mythology: an essay*. A. Smythe Palmer (ed). London: George Routledge & Sons. First published in his *Oxford Essays* (1856).

from the Beacon to Carn Brea". In many ways, Hunt's ground breaking research set a benchmark for subsequent folklore collectors in the British Isles. It also created a wide audience for Cornish folklore, and along with Bottrell's *Traditions and Hearthside Stories of West Cornwall*, it ensured a prominent place for traditional narrative, and for giant tales in particular, in am emerging sense of Cornish distinctiveness.[25, 26]

Cornwall endured huge social change throughout the nineteenth century. Widespread hunger resulted in food riots, to which Cornwall was particularly prone. A third of the population emigrated, and the pace of industrial development devastated the landscape and caused thousands of casualties. At the same time, the opening of Brunel's great bridge at Saltash in 1859 and the gradual incursion of the railways, were beginning to bring further cultural and economic change, (though Cornish isolation may have been exaggerated in the past).[27] Some economic and political changes were perceived in Cornwall as being discriminatory, even when it came to extending the franchise:

> The uniform £10 householder qualification was designed as a rough and ready measure of borough enfranchisement for those with sufficient property to be trusted with the vote. In higher rated London working class voters were not uncommon; in remote Cornwall or parts of Wales even some shopkeepers failed to qualify.[28]

As at the imposition of the English Prayer Book three hundred years before (which the Cornish rejected in the famous words: "We, the Cornish men, where of certain of us understand no English, utterly refuse this new English") cultural challenge produced a new assertion of Cornish identity, which took a variety of forms. In the

25 Dorson, Richard (1968). *The British Folklorists: A History*. London, Routledge and Kegan Paul, p. 323.
26 Bottrell, William (1870–80). *Penzance*, reprint Llanerch (1996).
27 See for instance Collins, Wilkie (1851). *Rambles beyond Railways*.
28 Evans, Eric J. (1983). *The Forging of the Modern State: Early Industrial Britain 1783–1870*. London, Pearson, p. 185.

circumstances of the time, political and military resistance were impossible, but eventually Cornwall did assert its independence by turning away from the Church of England to Methodism, the only region in southern Britain to do so in substantial numbers.[29] The high number of food riots might also indicate an autonomist component which could not easily be articulated in Victorian Cornwall.[30] Such feelings were certainly powerfully present in early modern times, as the Tudor rebellions attest, and as Richard Carew noted in his 1602 *Survey of Cornwall*:

> … together with the Welsh, their ancient countrymen, namely, now fostering a fresh memory of their expulsion long ago by the English, they second the same with a bitter repining at their fellowship, and this the worst sort express in combining against and working them all the shrewd turns which with hope of impunity they can devise.[31]

Mark Stoyle's books too, reveal the extent to which a sense of national identity shaped Cornwall's role in the Civil War, and on into the nineteenth century, in the writings of R S Hawker of Morwenstow, for instance.[32]

To a large extent the nineteenth century world was shaped by nationalism. The American Revolution took place in 1783 and the French defeat of the Austrians in 1797 allowed smaller nations to emerge from the shadows of Empire,

---

29 Evans, Eric J., *op. cit.*, p. 268.

30 For the Prayer Book Rebellion, see Payton, Philip (2004). *Cornwall: A History*. Fowey, Cornwall Editions, pp. 120–26. And Rowse, A. L. (1941). *Tudor Cornwall: Portrait of a Society*. London, Jonathon Cape, pp. 253–90; for tw very different views.

31 Carew, Richard (1602). *Survey of Cornwall*. Reprint Redruth, Tamar Books (2000).

32 Stoyle, Mark (2002). *West Britons: Cornish Identities and the Early Modern British State*. Exeter, University of Exeter. And Stoyle, Mark (2005). *Soldiers and Strangers: An Ethnic History of the English Civil War*.

... and whatever else it was, 1848, the "springtime of peoples" was clearly also, and in international terms primarily, an assertion of nationality, or rather of rival nationalities. Germans, Italians, Hungarians, Poles, Romanians and the rest asserted their right to be independent and unified states embracing all members of their nations against oppressive governments, as did Czechs, Croats, Danes and others, though with growing misgivings about the revolutionary aspirations of bigger nations which seemed excessively ready to sacrifice their own.[33]

Indeed, smaller national groups ruled by the more successful imperial states often fared badly. Ireland, for instance, lost half its population and much of its ancient culture due to starvation and emigration during the famine years, and even little Cornwall suffered from mass emigration during the "Hungry Forties" and beyond, hence the frequent food riots, in Helston, Penzance and elsewhere. Though nationalism was indeed a powerful force, its precise form of expression depended on local circumstances.

The Cornish Revival

But interest in Cornish history, language, and culture did grow throughout the century. Polwhele's seven-volume *History of Cornwall* was published in 1816, and there were others. In 1826 Davies Gilbert published John Keigwin's version of *Pascon agan Arluth*, ("The Poem of Mount Calvary").[34] Edwin Norris's edition of the *Ordinalia*, the medieval Cornish masterpiece, came out in two volumes in 1859,[35] and attempts were made to gather the fragments of the Cornish language which remained, by Charles Roger of Stonehowle supported by the Royal Cornwall Polytechnic Society, Thomas

33 Hobsbawm, Eric (1975). *The Age of Capital 1848–1875*. London, Weidenfeld and Nicholson. Reprint Abacus (2000), pp. 103–4.

34 Davies, Gilbert (1826). *Mount Calvary Interpreted in the English Tongue by John Keigwin*. London, Nichols.

35 Norris, Edwin (1859). *The Ancient Cornish Drama*. Two volumes, Oxford, Oxford University Press. See also Bakere, Jane A (1980). *The Cornish Ordinalia: A Critical Study*. Cardiff, University of Wales Press.

Quiller-Couch, Lord Mount Edgcumbe and others.[36] As elsewhere in Europe, cultural self-assertion could develop political implications, and the career of Henry Jenner, the founder of the Cornish language revival illustrates this.

Of Jenner, his fellow language revivalist A S D Smith ("Caradar") wrote:

A'n Dasserghyans Kernewek ev o tas / mur y gerensa dhe Gernow y wlas. / Py fen-ny, na-ve ef ha'y weres bras?

To the Cornish Revival he was a father / great was his love for Cornwall his land. / Where would we be but for him and his great help?[37]

Jenner was born at St Columb Major in 1848, the year of revolutions. In 1851 the family moved to south east England, where Jenner grew up, In 1870 he became Junior Assistant in the Manuscript Department at the British Museum, which seems to have stimulated his philological interests, and in 1873 he read his paper "The Cornish Language" to the Philological Society. In 1875 he toured West Cornwall with W S Lach-Szyrma collecting Cornish language vocabulary. He presented his findings to the Philological Society in 1876. Later he discovered the Cornish "Charter Fragment" at the British Museum. Busy decades as a scholar and administrator followed, and in 1901 he became Vice-President of the new Cowethas Kelto—Kernuak, Celto—Cornish Society. His ground-breaking *Handbook of the Cornish Language* followed in 1904. Though few people can ever have learned to speak Cornish from Jenner's *Handbook*, it was the first serious attempt to systemize the language, and was therefore the true beginning of the language revival.[38] It apparently lost money, but Jenner was pleased to get a favourable response from clerks, small businessmen, shopkeepers and work-men—those he described as "the classes that form the backbone of

36 Berresford, Ellis, pp. 125−46.

37 Saunders, Tim (1991), *The Wheel: An Anthology of Modern Poetry in Cornish 1850−1980*. London, Francis Boutle, p. 77. My translation.

38 Jenner, Henry (1904). *A Handbook of the Cornish Language. Chiefly in its Latest Stages*

Cornish Methodism". The book thus appealed to the least anglicized (and Anglicanized) section of the population. And in addressing the question of language revival, Jenner linked it to the issue of national identity:

> Why should Cornishmen learn Cornish? There is no money in it, it serves no practical purpose, and the literature is scanty and of no great originality or value. The question is a fair one, the answer is simple. Because they are Cornish.[39]

The connection became still more explicit when, in the same year as the *Handbook*'s publication, Jenner delivered his speech, "Cornwall: A Celtic Nation" to the Celtic congress which finally led to Cornwall's admission to that body. Cornwall was a nation once again.[40, 41]

Perhaps the most enduring and popular symbol of Cornishness to emerge from the nineteenth century resurgence was Hawker's rousing ballad, "Song of the Western Men", an outstanding example of the then popular historical ballad genre. Though a Devon man by birth Hawker acquired a deep love of Cornwall through his Cornish wife and his long years as a parish priest at Morwenstow.[42] Much as his literary work was inspired by Cornish history and legend and though his "Song of the Western Men", often called "Trelawny", seems to be unhistorical, it has acquired the status of a Cornish national anthem. His other work is less well known, but:

with some Account of its History and Literature. London, D Nutt. Revised edition (2010), Cathair na Mart: Evertype.ISBN 978-1-904808-37-4

39 Williams, Derere R. (2004). *Henry and Katherine Jenner. A Celebration of Cornwall's Culture, Language and Identity*. London, Francis Boutle, pp. 98–9.

40 See Deacon, Bernard, Dick Cole, and Garry Tregigda (2003). *Mebyon Kernow and Cornish Nationalism*. Cardiff, Welsh Academic Press, p. 14–15.

41 Chapter on "Robert Stephen Hawker of Morwenstow", in Rowse, A. L. (1986). *The Little Land of Cornwall*. London, Alan Sutton, pp. 247–77.

42 Kent, Alan M. (2000). *The Literature of Cornwall: Continuity, Identity, Difference, 1000–2000*. Bristol, Redcliffe Press. See also Brendon, Piers (1975). *Hawker of Morwenstowe*. London, Cape.

As a poet recounting and reinterpreting a pre-industrial age in an industrial one, Hawker has come to embody the essence of Cornish patriotism.[43]

Mark Stoyle has argued that Hawker consciously manipulated Cornish history "to inspire a return to the good old Cornish values", and to turn back the clock to the day before John Wesley had "corrupted and degraded the Cornish character", from Hawker's own High Church perspective. In this sense he represents a continuation or revival of the Cornish identity of the Royalist Army in the Civil War, under the leadership of men like Sir Bevill Grenville, who was a particular hero of Hawker's and inspired one of his best ballads.[44] This brand of romantic nationalism contributed to the creation of a more hard-edged political movement in the twentieth century.[45]

Right across Europe, folklore too played its part in the formation of new "imagined communities". Organic views of development linked the growing folklore collection to notions of national character, in the work of the Finnish scholar Lönnrot for instance; who compiled the collections of Karelian stories published in 1835. More influential still were the two volumes of *Kinder-und Hausmärchen* ("Children's and Household Tales") published by Jakob and Wilhelm Grimm in 1812 and 1815.[46] The Grimm's methodology was widely copied, and was closely linked to the ideological position that the folklore of a people was uniquely expressive of its particular history and characteristics. The Grimms themselves came to believe this, and their views influenced other collectors such as the Norwegians, Asbjørnsen and Moe.[47] In Britain, Hunt and Bottrell

---

43 Stoyle, Mark (2002). *West Britons: Cornish Identities and the Early Modern British State*. Exeter, University of Exeter Press, pp. 175–80.

44 See Deacon, Cole, and Tregidga, *op. cit.*, Chapter 11 "The Historical Legacy: Nationalism before MK", pp. 14–25.

45 Georges, Robert and Michael Owen Jones, (1995). *Folkloristics: An Introduction.* Bloomington, Indiana University Press, pp. 36–40.

46 Davidson, Hilda Ellis and Anna Chaudhri (2003). *A Companion to the Fairy Tale.* Cambridge, O S Brewer, p. 8.

47 Bottrell, *op. cit.*, First series, p. 6.

were at the forefront of the folklore movement, and they both placed Cornish identity at the heart of their concerns. In series one of his *Traditions and Hearthside Stories of West Cornwall*, Bottrell, who even describes himself as "an old Celt", commits himself to telling the tales of West Cornwall, "the inhabitants of which are also distinguished by peculiar traits of character" and, like Hunt at the forefront of these stories he places the giant stories.

> From the dwellers in the lonely hamlets of the northern parishes have been obtained all the giant stories, and many weird legends belonging to this wild district.[48]

Insofar as folklore was an essential component of the emerging national project, giants were the key to its symbolic success.

Many of the Cornish giant stories involve the overthrow, and murder of what is often described as an "old" giant. Most of the aboriginal British giants were killed by Brutus and his Trojans, though some lingered on in Cornwall, whose new ruler, Corineus, killed the giant Gogmagog in a wrestling match at Plymouth (thus inaugurating Cornish wrestling). At Treryn Castle, "an ancient British fortress", there was a band of giants. A young giant had an affair with the leader's wife, and stabbed the old giant in the belly as he sat dozing in the giant's chair, then threw him into the sea. The giant lovers took possession of Treryn and lived there happily for many years.[49] The giant of Nancledry was a solitary misanthrope who ate children, as did the giant Trebigean: antipathy between the "old" giant and young men or boys seems to have been common. Tom kills the giant Blunderbuss and inherits his castle, his wealth and his wife, as we have already seen. The giant of Morva died and left twenty sons to inherit his estate, and a feast was founded in his memory. St Agnes was driven to kill Bolster to escape his lust, and in a similar story at Goran, an anonymous cannibal giant is tricked and killed by a "doctor". The killing is commemorated in the name of the local promontory, the Dodman or "dead man".

---

48 Hunt, *op. cit.*, p. 48.

49 Hunt, *op. cit.*, p. 53.

Totem and Taboo

Freud's seminal book *Totem and Taboo* was published in 1913, and its principal theme is the Oedipus complex, which Freud called "The Nuclear Complex" of the neuroses.[50] Freud placed it at the heart of his psychology and at the heart of our culture, as Peter Gay has said:

> Sibling rivalries, tensions between mothers and daughters, or fathers and sons, death wishes against family members, all seem wicked and unnatural. They offend the most highly prized official pieties but, Freud drily observed, they are no secret to anyone. The Oedipus Complex, embodied in myths, tragedies and dreams no less than in daily life, is implicated in all these closet conflicts. It is driven into the unconscious, but is all the more consequential for that.[51]

Freud also saw the Oedipus theory as an "attempt to dig down to the most remote foundations of culture",[52] and he often thought of himself as an archaeologist of the soul. He told his client, in the famous case of the "wolf man", that:

> The psychoanalyst, like the archaeologist in his excavations, must uncover layer after layer of the patient's psyche, before coming to the deepest, most valuable treasures.[53]

In this respect he modelled himself on Heinrich Schliemann, the great German discoverer of the site of Troy.[54] Freud thought the career of Schliemann so extraordinary because in discovering "Priam's Treasure", he had found true happiness. "There is happiness only," he wrote, "as fulfilment of a child's wish"; and he

---

50 Freud, Sigmund (1955) (1913). "Totem and Taboo and other works". *Standard Edition of the Complete Psychological Works*. Vol XIII (1913–14). London, Hogarth Press and the Institute of Psychoanalysis.

51 Gay, Peter (1988). *Freud: A Life for our Time*. London, Dent, p. 112.

52 Gay, *op. cit.*, p. 324.

53 Gay, *op. cit.*, p. 171.

54 See Traill, David (1995). *Schliemann of Troy: Treasure and Deceit*. London, Penguin.

41

often used archaeology as a metaphor for psychoanalysis, in his preface to the famous "Dora" case for instance.[55] Seeing himself as a "Schliemann of the mind", Freud drew on the work of Frazer, Robertson Smith, Tylor and Darwin to explain the Oedipus complex, the "hidden treasure that lay at the heart of the human psyche". In doing so he linked past with present, in both content and methodology, and the link was the "Little Hans" case, which linked animal phobia in the present to unresolved Oedipal material buried in the unconscious.

And to do this he told a story. Drawing on Darwin's conjecture that early human societies were composed of small, familial hordes, Freud imagined an original group of brothers getting together to kill and eat the fierce jealous ruler of the horde, the father.[56] In doing so they put an end to the patriarchal horde itself, and made a beginning of human history. And having killed the father they ate him:

> Cannibalistic savages as they were, it goes without saying that they devoured their victim as well as killing him. The violent primal father had doubtless been the feared and envied model of each of the company of brothers; and in the act of devouring him they accomplished their identification with him, and each one of them acquired a portion of his strength. The totem meal which is perhaps mankind's earliest festival, would thus be a repetition and a com-memoration of this memorable and criminal deed, which was the beginning of so many things—of social organization, of moral restrictions and of religion.[57]

As often in Freud the precise status of this theory is unclear: he himself seems to have believed it reflected a real prehistoric event, but this is of course untestable. It is perhaps most fruitfully viewed as a myth of origin, of the type which is commonly found in mythologies across the globe. It is also to be found in the giant stories

---

55 See Gay, *op. cit.*, p. 174.

56 See Gay, *op. cit.*, pp. 329−3. Also, Desmond, Adrian and Moore, James (1991). *Darwin*. London, Michael Joseph

57 Freud, *op. cit.*, p. 142.

of Cornwall, and the many parallels between Freud's myth and Hunt and Bottrell's will be evident. In the first place, the Cornish giants are often "cannibal savages", as we have seen, and though cannibalism on the part of their killers may have been repressed or censored by storytellers (in much the same way as the individual "represses" murderous Oedipus impulses directed at his own father), memories of it may be present in the traditional Morvah Feast, described by Margaret Courtney, and perhaps also in the Bolster Day Carnival, invented in the early 1990s, which features a large effigy of the giant and takes place over May Bank Holiday weekend.[58, 59] The primal cannibal feast (the devouring of the father) was, as we have seen, the beginning of religion and culture in Freud's view, and in the stories too, apart from the institution of feasts and carnivals, we often see that the death of the giant is a catalyst for change and innovation. Corineus's tussle with Gogmagog was the origin of Cornish wrestling, and Tom's encounter with Jack the Tinkeard, after he has killed Blunderbuss, leads to the learning of new skills, such as ploughing, brewing and the mining of tin.[60] The title of Hunt's story, "Tom the Giant, and his wife Jane, and Jack and the Tinkeard",[61] implies that, after killing Blunderbuss, Tom himself becomes a giant, or perhaps that he was one all along. In any case, he inherits the giant's land and treasures, and becomes his symbolic son in terms of the narrative structure. In the Cornish stories too, as if in fulfilment of the Oedipal fantasy, the giant killer inherits the giant's widow.[62] In both Freud's and Hunt's stories the death of the giant inaugurates a new age, a transition from the primitive to the civilized, the inception of the arts which make culture possible. The Cornish giant myth thus expresses Freud's seminal "family romance", the bedrock, in his view, of both individual psychology and culture.

---

58 Courtney, *op. cit.*, p. 51–2.

59 See Deane and Shaw, *op. cit.*, p. 155.

60 See Hunt, Robert, *op. cit.*, pp. 66–72.

61 Hunt, Robert, *op. cit.*, p. 60.

62 As in the story of the rival giants of Treryn, for instance, Hunt p. 48; and we recall that Tom married Blunderbuss's widow Jane.

The Oedipal theory has of course been critiqued from various perspectives. Malinowski, for instance, denied its existence among matrilineal peoples, such as the Trobriand islanders,[63] and post-Freudian and feminist critics have read the story differently, emphasizing the rivalrous anger of fathers towards their sons, and the girl's attempt to resolve the Oedipus Complex. If these critics are right, then the theory itself may be a social construct.[64] Why then did this story come to prominence in the nineteenth century Cornwall, and what purposes did it serve?

Audience and Identity

The issue is complicated by questions of identity and audience, so we must first ask what was the intended audience for these stories? For as Žižek writes, "in order to interpret a scene or an utterance sometimes, the key thing to do is to locate the true addressee".[65] Both Hunt and Bottrell wrote with the intention of preserving what remained of a tradition which was felt to be dying, and of validating that tradition by presenting it to an educated audience outside the Duchy itself. As Hunt says in his introduction to the *Popular Romances*:

> Hoping to have been successful in saving a few interesting fragments of the unwritten records of a peculiar race, my labours are submitted to the world.[66]

Hunt and Bottrell are thus attempting to present and interpret Cornish folklore to "the world", in this context, educated Englishmen, who had begun to visit Cornwall in increasing numbers,

---

63 Malinowski, Bronsiław (1926). "The Role of Myth in Life" *Psyche*, Vol 24. But see also Dundes, Alan (1984). *Sacred Narrative: Readings in the Theory of Myth*. University of California Press.

64 See, for instance, Barkan, David (1996). *The Duality of Human Existence: Isolation and Communication in Western Man*. New York, Beacon Press. Chadorow, Nancy (1978). *The Reproduction of Mothering: Psychoanalysis and the Sociology of Gender*. Berkeley, University of California Press. And Kristeva, Julia (1989). *Black Sun*. New York, Columbia University Press.

65 Žižek, Slavoj (2008). *In Defence of Lost Causes*. London, Verso, p. 82.

66 Hunt, Robert, *op. cit.*, p. 32.

due to the expansion of the railways and the development of tourism. As we have seen, folklore was widely used in the nineteenth century to fashion developing national identities.[67] This explains the occasionally apologetic or even mocking tone of some collectors (though this is not characteristic of Hunt), as they attempt to distance themselves from their informants and lay claim to the higher status of their readership.[68]

But the stories "in themselves" belong to the repertoire of the droll-teller; that is, they were told within the community, which was itself both audience and narrator, addressee and sender. And on that level, the stories must have made sense to the Cornish themselves, in terms of both their identity and their historical situation.

Oedipus, of course, is about identity, because it is the son's revolt against the father that enables him to become a man in his own right, much as Tom can only come into his inheritance after he has killed the giant. On an individual level, fairy tales help the child to make sense of these disturbances and the feelings that accompany them. As Bettelheim says:

The fairy tale suggests not only isolating and separating the disparate and confusing aspects of the child's experience into opposites, but projecting these into different figures. Even Freud found no better way to help make sense out of the incredible mixture of contradictions which co-exist in our mind

---

67 See also Schacker, Jennifer (2003). *National Dreams*. Philadelphia, University of Pennsylvania Press.

68 Howells, in his 1831 *Collection of Welsh Folklore* writes: 'We rejoice that the beatific rays of wisdom have gleamed through the dark clouds of ignorance and superstition... and the march of intellect has made its appearance, even amongst the mountains and velleys of Wales'. Others such as Jeremiah Curtin in his 1890 book, took refuge in an ironic style, as did Bottrell. The stories were being sent up, even as they were being preserved. See Howells, W (1831). *Cambrian Superstitions*. Reprinted Llanerch (1991). Curtin, Jermia (1890. *Myths and Folklore of Ireland*. Reprinted Random House (1996). And McMahon, Brendan (2009). *Cornish Folklore: The Nineteenth Century Background*. An Baner Kernewek, 138.

and inner life than by creating symbols for isolated aspects of the personality. He named them id, ego and superego.[69]

Might it not be that on a communal level too, the stories helped the Cornish to deal psychologically with the drastic challenges to their identity posed by nineteenth century capitalism, which must have aroused profound anxieties, even if Alan Kent discerns in the literature of the period "an outstanding vision of industrial confidence and revival identity".[70] Thus the Oedipal story is transformed from a personal into a communal myth told in a social setting, linking the contemporary community to its past, and affirming its continuity as much as psychoanalysis shapes the structure of the psyche itself etc superego, ego, id, one of the truly "big narratives" of the twentieth century, in the western world and beyond.

III

The Knockers

The supernatural entity most closely associated with Cornish industrialization is the Knocker. Knockers or knackers were also known as buccas, though this term is more extensive. They were spirits who inhabited the mines and helped the miners by warning of danger and drawing attention to profitable lodes of tin.[71] Knockers were short, gnome-like figures, "miserable little, old, withered dried-up creatures, the tallest of them no more than three foot six".[72] In some respects these resemble the gnomes of Germanic tradition, in others they seem to have been particularly adapted to the Cornish system of "tribute" mining (under which the men worked for a percentage of the value of the ores in lieu of wages).[73]

---

69 Bettelheim, Bruno (1976). *The Uses of Enchantment: The Meaning and Importance of Fairy Tales*. Harmondsworth, Penguin, p. 75

70 Kent, Alan M., *op. cit.*, p. 104.

71 Simpson and Roud, *op. cit.*, pp. 205–6.

72 Bottrell,, *op. cit.*, p. 188.

73 Jenkin, A. K. Hamilton (1927). *The Cornish Miner*. London, Allen and Unwin, p. 134.

Mining has taken place in Cornwall since ancient times, though by the time Hunt's *Popular Romances* were published it was in decline, bringing starvation and large scale emigration in its wake:

The metalliferous mining industry of Cornwall was one of extreme antiquity; industrialization took place relatively early in the eighteenth century... by the mid-nineteenth century Cornwall was supplying almost one third of the world's tin and copper. Thirty years later the development of overseas ore deposits had rendered Cornwall's output negligible, a decline marked in Cornwall by abandoned and closed mines and "clemmed" (starving) mineworkers.[74]

The history of the knockers paralleled the history of Cornish mining. According to Hunt, "there is scarcely a spot in Cornwall where tin is at present found, that has not been worked over by the "old men", as the ancient miners are always called."[75] It was widely believed that they were the spirits of Jews, condemned to work forever for their part in the crucifixion of Christ (like Tregeagle's endless tasks, a punishment for sin, and a potential route to salvation), though paradoxically they were believed to celebrate Mass in the deepest shafts on Christmas Eve.[76] Tin is linked to Cornwall's Catholic past in other ways. Saint Piran or Perran, who may be identical with the Irish Saint Ciarán, was the patron saint of mining, whose cult was also popular in Britanny and South Wales.[77] The saint's feast day on the 5th of March was kept as a holiday by the tinners well into the nineteenth century, and his cross, symbolizing the white tin emerging from the black soil, and the grace

74 Burke, G (1984), "The Cornish Diaspora of the Nineteenth Century". In Marks, Shula, and Peter Richardson (1984). *International Labour Migration: Historical Perspectives*. Hounslow, Maurice Temple-Smith/University of London, pp. 57–75.

75 Hunt, Robert, *op. cit.*, p. 341.

76 Hunt, Robert, *op. cit.*, pp. 349–50.

77 See John, Catherine Rachel (1981). The Saints of Cornwall. Redruth, Dyllansow Truran, pp. 52–3. And Tomlin, E. W. F. (1982). *In Search of St Piran*. Padstow, Lodenek.

of God triumphing over evil and ignorance, is now widely recognized as a symbol of Cornish identity.

It was widely believed that the Phoenicians had visited Cornwall to buy tin, and even that Saint Paul purchased tin at Creekbraws, which was still a working mine in Hunt's time. The great apostle was said to have preached at Gwennap. which hosted the annual Methodist convocation in his honour. In east Cornwall the tinners celebrated, on the second Thursday before Christmas, the feast of Saint Picrous, of whom nothing else is known.[78]

In the extraordinary droll of Jack the Tinkeard, Jack the epony-mous giant killer is depicted as a culture hero who brings the knowledge of tin to Cornwall, an event which is still commemorated at Morva Fair.[79] William Bottrell's re-telling of the story of Tom Trevorrow is firmly set in the context of Cornish history and culture:

Tom and the Knackers

Bottrell's informant for this story was "Uncle Bill", a Lelant miner who spoke in dialect, and in his introduction Bottrell complains of stories written "by strangers to the country", "in an uncouth jargon put into the mouths of West Country folks, which is no more the common dialect of Cornwall than it is of Jericho".[80] He goes on to praise the everyday English of "Cornish working people with its sprinkling of genuine old Cornish", and it is hard not to hear in this an elegy for the Cornish language itself. Belief in traditional lore is also associated with this "genuine old Cornish" speech:

> "Strangers," said Uncle Bill, "don't believe in the sperats we calls knackers workan in the bals (mines), and say it is all superstition! Now that's a fine word, my dear, and I may to use it on all occasions!"[81]

---

78 Hunt, Robert, *op. cit.*, p. 342.

79 Hunt, Robert, *op. cit.*, p. 72.

80 Bottrell, William, 1996 (1873). *Traditions and Hearthside Stories of West Cornwall.* Felinfach Llanerch Press, pp. 185–90.

81 Bottrell, *op. cit.*, p. 186.

This of course was a familiar problem for tellers of traditional stories in the nineteenth century; how to make their stories palatable to the middle-class, Received Standard English speaking audience, without seeming to endorse the "superstitious" worldview of alien cultures, which were often associated with Roman Catholicism and resistance to contemporary progressive views. So Hunt is obliged to praise John Wesley for helping to eradicate "superstition", so that, by his day, the knackers were seldom heard of:

> He found the country steeped in the darkness of superstitious ignorance, and he opened a new light upon it. Associated with the spread of Wesleyan Methodism, has been the establishment of schools; and under the influence of religion and education, many of the superstitions have faded away.[82]

In the latter half of the nineteenth century Cornish speech and folkways were being encroached upon by what was then the greatest power on earth and as a result we see the sense of insecurity and defensiveness which inevitably results: this is not entirely absent from twenty-first century representations of Cornwall and the Cornish. Bottrell neatly evades the issue by putting his own subversive thoughts into the mouth of "Uncle Bill", who begins the story of Tom and the Knackers.

Tom lived in Trecroben and worked in Wheal Reath. Then

> twenty years or so ago, when work fell slack here, and some bals were knacked (mines closed) he went to St Just and found work in Ballowal, that was worked before the flood they say… There the old men's works, just as they left them, only washed and ruind in a good deal, one may suppose. That old bal, everybody in Santust will tell 'e, have always been haunted with knackers, and with spriggans, wherever anything belonging to the old bal was burred. There these sprites keep everlastan watch.[83]

---

82 Hunt, Robert, *op. cit.*, p. 347.

83 "Spriggans" were guardian spirits.

Tom and his family moved to St Just to work in the bal, and he often heard the knackers working nearby. Irritated by the noise, Tom threw some pebbles in their direction, which were immediately thrown back. After working a bit longer, he sat down to eat his fuggan or cake, when he heard voices singing:

"Tom Trevorrow! Tom Trevorrow!
Leave some of thy fuggan for Bucca,
or bad luck to thee tomorrow!"[84]

But he disregarded the knackers' warning, ate his fuggan, and fell asleep. When he woke up, he saw that he was surrounded by the knackers. Old "Uncle Bill" continues:

One older and uglier than the rest—if possible—seemed to take the lead in makan wry faces and all sorts of mockan tricks. When he put his thumb to his nose and squinted at Tom, all those behind him did the same. Then all turned their backs, stooped doen, lolled out their tongues and grinned at him from between their spindly shanks.[85]

Tom was frightened, but the knackers disappeared, and when he told the other miners what had happened, they blamed him for not sharing his fuggan, "as et was an old custom". The next day was "Corpeus Chris", the old Catholic feast of the Blessed Sacrament, and Tom's son wanted to go to the fair at Penzance. Tom wanted his company at the mine, after his experience of the previous day, and promised to take him to the games on Midsummer's Day instead.

Midsummer was an important day in Cornwall, as in the ancient Celtic year, associated with lovemaking and divination, and the lighting of the famous midsummer bonfires, once defunct but revived in 1929 and popular to this day. Once the first fire was lit on the Garrack Sans, the "Holy Rock" near Sennen Cove, from which a chain of fires spread on Carn Brea, Sancreed Carn Marth and so

84 Bottrell, *op. cit.*, p. 186.

85 Bottrell, *op. cit.*, p. 188.

on, covering the length of Cornwall. Parades and street dancing took place in Penzance and other places, and Midsummer's Day itself, the feast of Saint John, was effectively a Cornish national holiday. Today at St Cleer the fire is topped with a witches hat and broom, and various other popular festivities have grown up around the date attesting to its deep roots in the Cornish past, and to the fact that it meets a deep psychological and emotional need for people to come together in community.[86] The Midsummer reference in Bottrell's story of "Uncle Bill" corresponds with the other affirmations of Cornish identity, the more so as it is followed by a defence of traditional Cornish sports:

> I don't see for my part why wrestlan, hurlan, and other old manlike games should be allowed to die out.[87]

Leaving home

There are so many affirmations of Cornish culture here that it hard not to see the story itself in that context. After all, Tom is punished for not sharing his food with the knockers, as tradition demands. Other stories have a similar message. Another of Hunt's *Romances of the Miners* hinges on the proverbial advice "Never leave an old road for a new one".[88] This story, "John of Chyanhor, or The Three Points of Wisdom" was written in Cornish by Nicholas Boson towards the end of the seventeenth century.[89] The hero of this story, which exists in different forms all over Europe, is a Cornishman forced to leave home in search of work,[90] a theme which must have had resonance in Hunt's day. Though Hamilton Jenkin has written of "the exodus of the 70s" following the copper crash of 1866, in fact,

---

86 Deane, Tony and Tony Shaw (2003). *Folklore of Cornwall*. Stroud, Tempus, pp. 160–1.

87 Bottrell, *op. cit.*, p. 189.

88 Hunt, Robert, *op. cit.*, pp. 344–6.

89 Padel, Oliver (1975). *The Cornish Writings of the Boson Family*. Redruth, Institute of Cornish Studies.

90 Kent, Alan M. (2000). *The Literature of Cornwall: Continuity, Identity, Difference 1000–2000*, p. 80–81.

emigration from Cornwall had been noticeable by the 1820s and was already a significant phenomenon by the 1830s and 1840s[91]

when Hunt was collecting his stories.

In a community which had recently lost its language and was losing its youngest and most energetic people, stories advocating the old beliefs and the old ways might well have a cohesive effect.

So Tom and his son went to the mine, and he was replacing some old timber when he heard the knockers and felt the ground move. He called out to his son to pull him up as the tunnel collapsed around him, and though he escaped with his life, he lost his tin. Other disasters followed, and eventually the knackers drove Tom out of the mine completely, and he was forced to work on a nearby farm, a real come-down for a tinner. One day his wife confided their troubles to a pellar or travelling magician, another important figure in traditional Cornish life.[92] He brought the family better luck and Tom returned to mining again. Tom's good luck continued, and his older boys went to America when they grew up:

> and they did so well over at Mineral Point, Galena or somewhere that way that they sent home enough to keep the old couple in comfort, and to bring the younger boys out to them, where they, with hundreds more from hereabout, are making another Cornwall for "one and all".

And with this hopeful vision of a new Cornwall across the western ocean, underlined by the old Cornish rallying cry "onen hag oll", the story comes to an end.

Of course, for most people emigration was driven by necessity rather than a romantic desire to recreate Cornwall overseas, though

91 Payton, Philip (1996). "'Reforming Thirties' and 'Hungry Forties: The Genesis of Cornwall's Emigration Trade", In Payton, Philip (ed) (1996). *Cornish Studies* 4. See also Steve Knightley's song "Cousin Jack", sung by Show of Hands on "Dark Fields" (1997).

92 See Jenkins, A. K. Hamilton (1933). *Cornwall and the Cornish*, pp. 109–72.

perhaps a desire to escape the tyrannies of the old world had something to do with it. Escape certainly became easier with the opening of the Saltash railway bridge, and soon "it was possible to book through to Houghton, Michigan from the general store in St Just".[93] The men went first and the families came after—Tom's family was not untypical—but they did not always find the peace they sought. Rowe has estimated that at least four or five thousand of the settlers of the Wisconsin region had emigrated there from Cornwall in the years between the ending of the Black Hawk war in 1832 and the discovery of gold in California in 1842—at which time many of them removed to the goldfields. In Montana from the 1880s the racial feud between Cornish and Irish was a fundamental part of the war of the copper kings. Marcus Daly employed only Irishmen at Anaconda, while William Clark employed only Cornishmen. These men came either directly from Cornwall or indirectly from the Comstock or California.[94]

That knockers or buccas were known long before Hunt's day is shown in the Middle Cornish play *The Creation of the World* based on the Book of Genesis, and rewritten by William Jordan in 1611, in which at one point Cain says dismissively of his brother Abel:

"My a'n syns gweth es bucca,
Ny won pyth eth dhe wandra."   1195

"I think him worse than a hobgoblin.
I don't know where he has gone astray."[95]

This fine play, originally written in the middle of the sixteenth century, was based on the earlier play in the *Ordinalia* cycle, dealing with the creation of the world. It was first translated into English by John Keigwin in the seventeenth or early eighteenth century, then by the great Irish scholar Whitley Stokes for the London Philological

---

93 Burke, *op. cit.*, pp. 59–60.

94 Burke, *op. cit.*, p. 59. See also Glasscock, C B (1938) *The War of the Copper Kings*. New York.

95 Hooper, E. G. Retallack (ed) (1985). *Gwryans an Bys or The Creation of the World*. Redruth, Dyllansow Truran.

Society in 1864.[96] The story of Adam and Eve and the Fall (1864) is of course at the heart of the Christian narrative, and foreshadows the divine mission of Christ, the "second Adam". As a result of their sin Adam and Eve are sent into exile in words that anticipate the exile of the Cornish miners and their families:

"Adam, ke yn-mes a'n wlas	971
dhe gres an bys dhe vewa:	
ty dha honen dhe balas,	
dha wrek genes dhe nedha."	974

"Adam, go out of the country
into the midst of the world to live:
thou thyself to dig,
thy wife with thee to spin."[97]

But God, after all their Tregeagle-like labours, gives his promise that:

"Adam, kens es deweth an bys,	938
my a wront Oyl Mercy dhys,	
ha dhe Eva dha wre'ty."	940

"Adam, ere the end of the world,
I will grant the Oil of Mercy to
thee, and to Eve thy wife."[98]

When Cain is accidentally slain in the play he is at first thought to be a "bucca", a metaphor which echoes folk belief about the knockers' ugliness (as in the description of "Uncle Bill"), but also perhaps medieval anti-Semitic views about the blood-guilt of the

---

96 Murdoch, Brian (1903). *Cornish Literature*. Cambridge, Boydec and Brewer, pp. 75−98. See also Ó Cróinín, Dáibhí (2011). *Whitley Stokes 1830-1909. The Lost Celtic Notebooks Re-discovered*. Dublin. Four Courts Press.

97 Hooper, *op. cit.*, pp. 71, trans R. Morton Nance and A. S. D. Smith.

98 Hooper, *op. cit.*, p. 69.

Jews, whose spirits the knockers were believed to be, views which were sadly prevalent across Europe during the Middle Ages:

"Yth 'valsa orth y favour	1587
y vos nep bucca-nos,	
ha henna y fyth prevys."	1589

"It would seem by its appearance
that it is some hobgoblin,
and that it will be proved."[99]

As the giants belonged to the rocky promontories, so the knockers belonged to the underground world, though they could occasionally make their presence felt elsewhere as in the following story which is of interest because it involves Hunt himself and because it includes a statement of authentic folk belief.

Robert Hunt and the Knockers

Somewhat paradoxically, after praising Methodism for helping to eradicate "superstition" in Cornwall, Hunt goes on to give evidence in support of traditional belief.[100] One Saturday night Hunt's daughters, two female servants, and "an old woman named Mary, who was left by the proprietor in charge of the house which I occupied", retired to bed. Hunt locked up the rented house and went to bed himself. After a while,

"I distinctly heard a bedroom door open, and footsteps which, after moving about for some time in the passage or landing, from which the bedrooms opened, slowly and carefully descended the stairs. I heard a movement in the kitchen below, and the footsteps again descended the stairs, and went into one of the bedrooms. This noise continued so long, and was so regularly repeated, that I began to fear lest one of the children were taken suddenly ill. Yet I felt assured,

---

99 Hooper, *op. cit.*, pp. 117−8.

100 For this and what follows, see Hunt, Robert, *op. cit.*, pp 347−89.

if it was so, one of the servants would call me. Therefore, I lay still and listened until I fell asleep."[101]

The next day Hunt inquired of the servants and his daughters, none of whom had left their rooms in the night or heard any noises. Eventually the younger servant Nancy confessed that the sound of men "threshing corn, and of beating the borer" (a mining term) was not uncommon in the house. Hunt asked Mary if it was the knockers he had heard the previous night. Mary confirmed that it was, carefully distinguishing between them and the malevolent spirits of the departed:

> Yes, 'twas the knackers working down upon the tin, no doubt of it… but none of the young ladies need be afraid. There are no spirits in the house; it is very nearly a new one, and no-one has ever died in the house.

Although the story begins with what sounds like the introduction to a conventional Victorian ghost story, it ends with these rather matter-of-fact words from a sensible Cornishwoman, to whom the "bucca" is just a fact of life. She represents the last generation for which that could have been said.

---

101 Hunt, Robert, *op. cit.*, p. 347.

Chapter 3

The Mermaid and the Saint

The Goddess and the Nymph

The image conjured up by the word "mermaid"—half-woman, half fish, the beautiful, seductive siren with her comb and mirror, was the creation of the classical world. The classical siren herself seems to have derived from the semitic moon goddess Atargatis, who personified the light and dark aspects of love. The second-century Greek writer Lucian saw a Phoenician image of her in the shape of a mermaid. The Greek identified Atargatis with Aphrodite, the goddess of love, and their word for "comb" also meant the female pudenda.[1]

In the worship of this goddess the sacred fish embodied the divine life of the waters, and she and her son were transformed into fishes. The same idea was expressed rather differently in the legend of the goddess who is born from the water, as Aphrodite was at Paphos.[2] Atargatis was a variant of the Great Mother who was worshipped from earliest times, under the names of Cybele, Isis, Aphrodite and Ishtar, and was believed to be bisexual. Under the name of Nina she received offerings of fish from her worshippers.[3] The Near Eastern goddess was borrowed by the Greeks and Romans and gradually developed into the nymphs and sirens of classical tradition, like the

---

1 Westwood, Jennifer and Jacqueline Simpson (2005). *The Lore of the Land*. London, Penguin, p. 20.
2 Mackenzie, Donald A. (1915). *Myths of Babylonia and Assyria*. London, Gresham, p. 28.
3 Mackenzie, *op. cit.*, p. 267.

ones which tempted Odysseus, and though she shed some of her grosser "eastern" attributes, she remained a temptress.[4]

From the classical world the lore of the siren travelled west during the course of the Middle Ages, when it merged with local traditions and took new forms. For preachers during this period she became an emblem of lust, a cautionary tale, a symbol of pagan hedonism as she had been in St Jerome's Vulgate.[5] (And one wonders whether this is the real significance of the famous mermaid bench-end in Zennor church.) Her comb and mirror became symbols of vanity and deadly allure, the seductive glamour of sin. Though, more positively, in the Cornish passion play the *Ordinalia*, she becomes a metaphor for the dual nature of Christ:

"He might be well half man and half God, human is half the mermaid woman from the head to the heart; so is the Jesus."
1. 1740-44[6]

As the "merrymaid" is both fish and woman, so is Christ both God and man, and a strongly Cornish image is used to express the heart of the Christian faith. Though in fact it seems likely that the mermaids of native tradition did not originally have the tails of fish; despite their magical powers they seem not to have been regarded as supernatural beings but as natural phenomena, and Hunt's informants seem to have regarded them in a rather matter-of-fact light.

"When, five and thirty years since, I spent several nights in a fisherman's cottage on a south-western coast, I was treated to many a 'long yarn' respecting mermaids seen by the father and his sons in the southern ocean. The appearance of those

---

4 See, for instance, Waterhouse's highly erotic "Hylas and the Nymphs".

5 Warner, Marina (1994). *From the Beast to the Blond*. London, Chatto and Windus, p. 113.

6 Quoted in Kent, Alan M. (2000). *The Literature of Cornwall: continuity, identity, difference 1000−2000 AD*. Bristol, Redcliffe Press, p. 38.

creatures on our own shores, they said, was rare; but still, they knew what they had seen."[7]

In fact, mermaid stories are to be found on all the Celtic coastlands, and they are also told of inland lakes and streams, at Chapel en le Frith and at Rostherne in Cheshire, for instance. Scotland has its "morroughs", Ireland its "merrows", and Cardigan Bay its mermaid.[8] The mermaids of the Isle of Man are particularly jealous and dangerous, though these are common traits.[9] Nor are these stories all located in a remote, legendary past. Over two or three summers in the 1890s a mermaid appeared regularly in Newark Bay in Orkney, and was seen by hundreds of people. It was described in a contemporary account as:

> … about six or seven feet in length, (with) a little black head, white neck, a snow-white body and two arms, and in swimming just appears like a human being. At times it will appear to be sitting on a sunken rock, and will wave and work its hands.[10]

The 1840s saw something of a vogue in mermaids, sparked off by Hans Christian Anderson's "The Little Mermaid" of 1837, in part inspired by Fouque's "Undine" and first translated into English in 1846. In part, Robert Hunt's *Popular Romances of the West of England* helped to popularize them here, and to create an association between mermaids and Cornwall which persists to this day, though his collection includes only three substantial mermaid stories. He prefaces his selection with a rather tantalizing reference to the mermaid lore of Morva, between Zennor and St Just, its stories of

---

7   Hunt, Robert (1881) 3rd edition. *Popular Romances of the West of England*. London, Chatto and Windus, p. 150

8   Spence, Lewis (1948). *The Minor Traditions of British Mythology*.

9   See, for instance, Broome, Dora (1963). *Fairy tales from the Isle of Man*. Douglas, Modern Press, pp. 21–29; and Moore, A. W., 1994 (1891). *The folk lore of the Isle of Man*. Felinfach, Llanerch Publishers, pp. 7–8.

10 Marwick, Ernest W. (2000). *The folklore of Orkney and Shetland*. Edinburgh, Bitlinn.

"ladies seen on the rocks" and "ladies sitting weeping and wailing on the shore";[11] but one has the impression that much material had already been lost.

The old man of Cury

"More than a hundred years since", on a fine summer's day, an old man from Cury was walking on the beach near Lizard Point when he came upon a beautiful fair-haired girl sitting on a rock and arranging her hair in her mirror. When he spoke to her she slid off the rock into the water, and he saw that she had a fish's tail instead of legs, though the rest of her body was concealed by her beautiful long hair. He spoke to her kindly, and she told him that she had been out swimming that morning with her husband and children, and had stopped to rest at Kynance Cove, where the merman had fallen asleep while she minded the children as they played on the sand. Attracted by the scent of flowers from over the cliff she floated from rock to rock, then paused to comb her hair and found she was stranded by the tide. She was frightened that her husband would eat the children if she did not return home soon:

> He was also dreadfully jealous, and if she was not at his side when he awoke, he would at once suspect her of having run off with some other merman.

She asked the old man to carry her back to the sea, which he did, and in return she granted his wish, which was to do good to his neighbours:

> … first, to break the spells of witchcraft; next to charm away diseases; and thirdly, to discover thieves, and restore stolen goods.

The mermaid agreed to meet him at the half-tide rock on another day to tell him how to accomplish his wish, then she gave him her comb, telling him to comb the water with it if he needed to summon

11 Hunt, Robert, *op. cit.*, p. 148.

her, and then she slipped off her rock and swam away, blowing him a kiss. On the appointed day the old man went to the half-tide rock (now called the Mermaid's Rock) and met the merrymaid, who instructed him how to break evil spells, discover thieves, charm away shingles, fetters, Saint Anthony's Fire and Saint Vitus Dance, and so on.

She persuaded him to take her to see "the funny people who had their tails split so they could walk", and offered to make him young again if he would come back to the sea with her, but he refused her offer. A local family has for generation possessed the powers of healing, passed down by the old fisherman, and is said to possess the mermaid's comb.[12]

Bottrell's version of the story features "a sober and staid married man near thirty years of age", rather than Hunt's "old fisherman", who has a conversation with the mermaid in the Cornish language. Though both storytellers emphasize that the maid is decently covered, they also emphasize her body as an object of desire, and in both stories she offers herself to her rescuer. This fits well with her divine origins as a goddess of love, and with the misogynistic medieval tradition. These traditions of course did not persist into nineteenth-century Cornwall, but the mermaid motif was clearly still available as a receptacle for sexual fantasies and projections. It is interesting too that the mermaid is associated with the past, and with the Cornish language and identity, now, like the mermaid herself, driven to the far west. In Bottrell's version her name is Morvena:

> "which, in the language of this part of the world, at the time
> I was named, meant 'sea woman'. You can't forget it,
> because you have still many names much like it among
> you."[13]

The subversive sexuality of the mermaid is evident in the folk tradition, (in the story of the mermaid at Zennor who lured the sweet-voiced chorister to his doom, for instance), and it occasionally

---

12 Hunt, Robert, *op. cit.*, pp 152–5.

13 Bottrell, William, 1996 (1870). *Traditions and Hearthside stories of west Cornwall.* 1st series, Felinfack, Llanerck Puplications.

found its way into Victorian art in, for instance, Herbert Draper's "Water Baby", painted in 1890 and now in the City of Manchester Art Galleries, in which an alluring young woman is desexualized by the maternal context and subtitled "A Good Mer-Mother". The idea that women might control their own sexuality was too dangerous. The mermaid at Zennor appeared as a normal woman when she seduced young Mathey Trewella, "the best singer in the parish" and was presumably able to engage in normal sexual relations. It was only later that she was seen in mermaid form and commemorated in the bench-end carving.[14] Perhaps the fishtail and long hair of some traditional stories also serves to defuse female sexuality, but there are also references to the mermaid's maternal instincts, in the story of the old man of Cury, for instance.

Yet despite all these defences against male anxiety the mermaid remained a wilful, independent young woman who knew her own mind, sexually and in other ways, and she could be possessive, jealous and vengeful, as in the story of the mermaid of Padstow, who choked up the harbour with sand after a local man shot at her; or in the tale told on the north coast but also on the Lizard.

The mermaid's vengeance
The style of this story is much more elaborate than Hunt's other mermaid tales, and at times it sounds more like a sensation novel by Wilkie Collins than a folk narrative.

In Perranzabulo there once lived a hard-working couple and their daughter. The man was called Pennaluna, or Penna the Proud by his neighbours, and he was a labourer on the farm of a wealthy man. Then he was appointed manager of an outlying farm, under the 'hind' or general farm supervisor, who was jealous of him and keen to find fault with his work. But Penna was always conscientious. Tom the hind had been attracted to Penna's wife Honour, who had rejected him, and he persecuted the Pennas in his resentment.

Their daughter Selina was very beautiful, and some said the fairies or the mermaids had made her so. She loved to walk along the beach

14 Bottrell, *op. cit.*, p. 288.

with her father, in all weathers, and in summer she bathed in the sea. Her mother complained that the girl didn't do enough housework, and pretended to be ill to get out of going to church. Many young men liked her but she kept them all at a distance.

Then a nephew of the squire, a young man called Walter who had been wounded in the wars, came home to recuperate. The young man was handsome but vain. He would often walk and bathe on the beach for his health, and so he became acquainted with Selina and her father. As he grew stronger he began to ride and shoot, with the help of Tom the steward, who had not forgotten his grudge against the Pennas, and encouraged Walter to seduce Selina; and the young man made friends with the girl's mother through flattery, eventually succeeding in seeing Selina on her own, when

> the witching whispers of unholy love were poured into her trusting ear.[15]

Tom induced the squire to send Penna to the Lands End to set to rights a repossessed farm there, and Walter took advantage of his absence to sleep with Selina, after which he abandoned her and went back to London.

When Penna returned he found his daughter pining away, and Tom spreading rumours that the Pennas had planned to trap Walter in a morganatic marriage. Penna responded angrily once the whole story reached the squire, who deprived Penna of his job and his cottage. In their new home Selina grew weaker and weaker, and was soon confined to her bed. Eventually, after apparently conversing with spirits, she died in childbirth.

Walter returned to Perran-on-the-Sands. Penna wanted to kill him, but "the good priest of the Oratory" dissuaded him. From then on everything went wrong for Tom Chenalls—his cows slipped their calves, his crops failed, his cattle died and his ricks burned. In his despair he turned to drink and lost his job. But he stayed friends with Walter and found him a cottage on the cliffs, and all the wild young men of the locality met there to drink.

---

15 Hunt, Robert, *op. cit.*, p. 151.

One night Walter was drinking there and went for a walk along the sands to cool his head, when he heard a woman singing sadly to her

angel child, my earth-born girl
From all your kindred riven
By the base deeds of a selfish churl
And to a sand grave driven.

He found the mermaid on a rock, and noticed her resemblance to Selina. She cursed him, and as he walked back along the beach, he heard the echoes of her laughter. He was filled with remorse for what he had done, and he wept over Selina's grave. The priest of the oratory comforted him, though he did not entirely believe his story. But from then on Walter was a changed man. He began to lose his health, and decided to return to the rock where he had met the mermaid. Again he heard her singing, but this time her song was a joyful one, and it seemed to him that the mermaid had Selina's face. "As you loved her so I love you," she said. "You are mine till death", and she embraced him as a storm broke above their heads. Carried away by the waves, he was drowned.[16]

This rather melodramatic story seems to have been influenced by the popular literature of the time, (the seduction of Selina is reminiscent of *David Copperfield*, for instance), but it also contains themes which are commonly found in the folk tradition. The style may give us a clue to what is really happening here. The traditional seductiveness of the mermaid is displaced on to her daughter Selina who is herself a victim of the conventional seducer Walter, and so the sanctity of Victorian womanhood is preserved, along with its passivity. Although the strong maternal feelings of the mermaid are expressed, so is her vengefulness, which explodes in rage at the end of the story. We find also a characteristically Victorian preoccupation with social class. Tom the steward is in part motivated by envy when he attempts to destroy the Pennas, declaring

16 Hunt, Robert, *op. cit.*, pp 155–70.

… that all people who kept themselves so much above other people were sure to be pulled down[17]

and it is Penna's upward mobility in the squire's service which arouses his envy, as well as his possession of Honour. Hunt's retelling of this traditional tale allows the exploration of very contemporary issues to do with social mobility and the role of women. Though aspects of the story, (the mermaid's song, the "priest of the oratory") suggest a remote, legendary period, this is also the modern world in which young men go out to fight in foreign wars, and men like Penna can make their way through energy and hard work. Even the repossessed farm at Land's End hints at current issues such as agrarian depression and emigration. But beneath this modern world lurk the ancient powers of love and hate, embodied in the enigmatic figure of the mermaid. In the end the enigma is a human one.

Hunt's story of the mermaid's vengeance is by far the fullest surviving account of its kind, and most of what remains is fragmentary. A mermaid west of Lamorna is said to sing before a storm, and at Seaton, near Looe, "a goodly commercial town" was overwhelmed by sand by the curse of a slighted mermaid.[18] Bottrell gives a slightly fuller account of Zennor's famous mermaid.

The Mermaid of Zennor
This story is told to account for the famous mermaid carving on a chancel seat at St. Senara's chcurch in Zennor. Though her hair is long and she proudly displays her magnificent tail, her stomach and breasts are revealed and her gaze is both challenging and unabashed; and she proudly displays her mirror and comb. Whether she is an invitation to sin or a warning against it is hard to say. Perhaps she can only evoke what is already there in the beholder. Her outstretched arms are both invitation and menace, and her story contains elements of both.

"Hundreds of years ago" a rich and beautiful lady attended St. Senara's church at irregular intervals, and the people were delighted

17 Hunt, Robert, *op. cit.*, p. 162.

18 Hunt, Robert, *op. cit.*, p. 152.

by her beauty and her sweet singing voice; though they wondered, as the years went by, how she managed to keep her good looks.

She grew friendly towards a young man called Mathey Trewella, who was "the best singer in the parish", and one day young Mathey followed her from church and never returned. After that the lady stopped attending church at Zennor.

One Sunday morning a ship cast anchor off Pendower Cove, and a mermaid swam up and hailed the captain. She said she was returning from church, and asked him to raise his anchor, which was blocking the entrance to her home. When the Zennor people heard this, they realized that their beautiful lady was a mermaid, and had her image carved on their bench-end.[19]

In this story, we see the mermaid in her traditional, seductive role, with the chorister taking the place of the customary handsome fisher lad. Her role as a rich lady reverses the Victorian theme of the rich man seducing the poor working girl, but also expresses the traditional assertiveness of the mermaid, in contrast to the feminine passivity which appealed so strongly to Victorian men.

It would seem that gender relations were changing in contemporary Cornwall, and it may be that the mermaid stories are an attempt to accommodate this. Bernard Deacon described how:

work on the smallholding or potato allotment or excursions to collect furze involved women as well as men and produced a distinct set of gender relations. The expansion of copper mining had led to the employment of young unmarried women at the surface works...

The spell of economic independence between childhood and marriage gave women in the mining districts a taste for economic and social independence symbolized by conspicuous spending on clothes and, it is argued, a lack of deference towards men."[20]

19 Bottrell 1996 (1873). *Traditions and Hearthside Stories of West Cornwall*. 2nd series, Felinfach, Llanerch Publications, p. 288.
20 Deacon, Bernard (2007). *Cornwall: a Concise History*. Cardiff, University of Wales Press.

This may have given a particularly Cornish slant to Victorian male anxieties about independent, sexual women.[21] Indeed, if Freud was right about the fundamental importance of the castration complex, then such anxieties may be universal.[22] It is easy to see that the mermaid's desirability, sexual voraciousness and lack, or apparent absence of genitalia could elicit a very ambivalent sexual response.[23] The story of Cherry, also set in Zennor, also deals with a love affair between a human and an otherworldly being but in that case it ends unhappily.[24]

Another tension embodied in the mermaid is that between killing and healing, life and death, and we have already seen her capacity for violence in "The Mermaid's Vengeance". In classical tradition mermaids sang sailors to sleep, then drowned or ate them; and we recall that the stranded mermaid in "The Old Man of Cury" was frightened that her husband would eat the children. Discussing an eerie incident described by Hunt, the appearance of a black figure on the hilltop, pausing briefly before running down Porthtowan beach, and disappearing into the sea, a story found "all around the Cornish coast". Payton observes:

> The interpretation is simple: that the sea-god, which provides and sustains life, demands perpetual sacrifice—a permanent and inevitable role, the burden and obligation of fishing and sea-faring communities who will always lose from amongst their number those called to appease the sea-god… This imperative may also inform Cornish mermaid stories, such as those of Seaton, Padstow, Lamorna and, most famously, Zennor.[25]

---

21 See, for instance, Silver, *op. cit.*; and Duffy, Maureen (1972). *The Erotic World of Faery*. London, Hodder and Stoughton.

22 See, for instance, Freud, Sigmund (1908). *On the Sexual Theories of Children*. Standard edition IX, pp. 215–16.

23 In the 1960s radio show "Round the Horne" Kenneth Horne described a mermaid as "the kind of girl you couldn't half have a good time with".

24 Hunt, Robert, *op. cit.*, pp. 120–126.

25 Payton, Philip (2004). *Cornwall: a History*. Fowey, Ian Grant, p. 21.

And indeed the sea-gods' demands were particularly evidenced in nineteenth-century Cornwall.[26] In Mount's Rose, for instance eleven ships and two hundred and fifty lives were lost between 1807 and 1811; and the village of Port Quis was said to have lost all its men in a storm at sea. Of course, many men engaged in seasonal fishing were also miners, and many of these young men and boys also died prematurely, through accidents, pulmonary disease and illness associated with poverty and malnutrition.[27]

Rivers and pools
But neither mermaids nor sudden death were confined to the coastal villages. As Katherine Briggs reminds us:

> The mermaid, in spite of her name, is not confined to the sea, but comes as far inland as the salmon, and is even to be found in lakes and ponds,[28]

and goes on to link the inland mermaid to such phenomena as the water bull, kelpies, and water horse. In Cornwall one might add the spirits of wells, streams and rivers. These inland mermaids, which represent the native tradition, in Britain generally

> lurked in rivers and ponds waiting to drown passers-by, especially children, just as mermaids of the sea drowned sailors.[29]

In this branch of the tradition, "mermaid" derives from Old English "mer", meaning "pool", modern English "mere". So in Cornwall "mermaids" were always "merry maids", though the first element in the equivalent Cornish word "morvoren" does mean

26 Rowe, John 1993 (1953). *Cornwall in the age of the Industrial Revolution*. 2nd edition. St Austell, Cornish Hillside Publications, pp. 200−4.

27 Rowe, John, *op. cit.*, pp. 312−14

28 Briggs, Katherine (1967). *The fairies in English tradition and literature*. London, Routledge and Kegan Paul, p. 41.

29 Westwood and Simpson, *op. cit.*, p. 696.

"sea". Grendel's mother, the fearsome monster in the Anglo-Saxon poem "Beowulf" is a "merewif", and she and her hideous son

> "are fatherless creatures... and their whole ancestry is hidden in a past of demons and ghosts. They dwell apart among wolves on the hills, on windswept crags and treacherous recesses, "where cold streams pour down the mountain and disappear under mist and moorland."[30] (11, 1355–61 *trans* S. Heaney)

In this poem the original pagan narrative has been placed in a Christian context, and the monsters are said to be the heirs of Cain, and of his guilt for the murder of his brother.[31] There are hints that something similar may have happened to the mermaids of oral tradition. Selina, in "The Mermaid's Vengeance" is criticized for not attending church (though the "Mermaid of Zennor" seems to be a regular communicant). Opinion as to their ultimate destiny seems to have been divided, as with the fairies: the Scots believed that mermaids were saved, while the Irish did not.[32] Another strand of tradition denies that mermaids possess souls, and asserts that their desire for union with human beings is motivated by this.[33] River spirits, generally personified as dangerous in Scotland and Ireland, are often named after a goddess; in many parts of the country the notion that the local river demands a quota of human sacrifice persists, and such stories are told of the Tweed, the Derwent and the Aire among others.[34]

From Lancashire, Cheshire and Shropshire comes the story of the water spirit, Jenny Greenteeth, who would drag unaware children

---

30 Heaney, Seamus (2010). *Beowulf: a verse translation*. London, Folio, p. 95.

31 See Tolkien, J. R. R. (1936). "The monsters and the critics", in Nicholson, Lewis E (1963). *An anthology of Beowulf criticism*. Notre Dame, University of Notre Dame Press.

32 Briggs, Katherine (1976). *A Dictionary of Fairies*. London, Allen Lane, pp. 287–290.

33 This belief is found in native Canadian stories. See, for instance, Rappoport, Angela 1995 (1928). *The Sea: Myths and Legends*. London, Senate, p. 166.

34 See, for instance, Hull, Eleanor (1928). *Folklore of the British Isles*. London, Methuen, pp. 57–58. Spence, *op. cit.*, pp. 11–24.

into pools and devour them.[35] Peg Powler, a spirit of the River Tees, behaved similarly, as did Peg O'Nell on the banks of the Ribble, though she is rationalized as a vengeful ghost who claims a life every seven years.[36] A headless stone in the grounds of Waddow Hall is said to represent her. Black Annis from Leicestershire was a similarly grim figure, though no association with water seems to be present. Legend has it that she later repented her sins and became a nun, and that there is a picture of her in Swithland Church.[37] The stone image of Peg O'Nell at Waddow is also said to represent some unknown saint.

The waters of life

Water spirits across the British Isles then are predominantly destructive, even murderous, and we have seen that mermaids also can share these characteristics. But as we have also seen, they are healers: in Robert Hunt's words

> Usually these creatures are associated with some catastrophe; but they are now and then spoken of as the benefactors of man[38]

and we have seen how the Laitey family in Cury received extraordinary healing powers from a mermaid. There is not very much of this in the Cornish tradition, though their Scottish sisters seem to have been more compassionate, as in the story of the Renfrewshire mermaid:

> who rose from the water as the funeral of a young girl passed, and said mournfully:
> "If they wad drink nettles in March
> and eat muggons in May,
> sae mony braw maidens
> wadna gang to the clay"

---

35 Simpson, Jacqueline and Steve Roud (2000). *A Dictionary of English Folklore*. Oxford, Oxford University Press, p. 199.

36 Simpson and Roud, *op. cit.*, p. 275.

37 Hull, Eleanir, *op. cit.*, p. 50.

38 Hull, Eleanir, *op. cit.*, p. 150.

Muggons is mugwort, or southern wood, and was much used for consumptive disorders. Mermaids had a great knowledge of herbs as well as prophetic powers.[39]

But healing is very much a part of the wider Cornish tradition. One healer, a "pellar" lived on the south coast and was famous for casting out devils from cattle and people, and for finding money that had been lost or stolen. He cured an "ill-wished" woman by instructing her to stick pins into a bullock's heart, while imagining that she was causing pain to the person who cursed her.[40] In all communities there are individuals who find it easy to believe that their neighbours wish them ill, and one can imagine that such harmless forms of therapy might be effective.

Holy wells

But in this context Cornwall is most famous for its holy wells and springs, which can bring spiritual as well as physical healing. As Hunt reflects:

> "Through all ages the fountains of the hills and valleys have claimed the reverence of men, and waters presenting themselves under aspects of beauty or of terror have been regarded with religious feelings of hope or of awe."[41]

And this seems to be literally true. Many of these sites, though sanctified by the medieval church and popular belief, are of pre-Christian origin, though some have been destroyed or desecrated due to changes in belief over the years:

> "the hearts of the people themselves have been slower to change, and their veneration of the holy wells, allied though it often was to superstition, remained until recently a very real force in their lives"[42]

---

39 Briggs, Katherine (1976). *A Dictionary of Fairies*. London, Allen Lane, p. 289.

40 Hunt, Robert, *op. cit.*, pp. 319–20.

41 Hunt, Robert, *op. cit.*, pp. 286–7.

42 Jenkins, A. K. Hamilton. (1933). *Cornwall and the Cornish: the story, religion and folklore of the western land*. London, J M Dent, p. 295.

and even today offerings are occasionally made at these holy places.[43] Fashions in belief and unbelief come and go, and Cornwall has been particularly troubled in that respect, but the need for supernatural help, especially when we are physically and psychologically vulnerable will always be with us. And this may have been particularly so in the mid-nineteenth century when mortality was so high, and the Methodist secession from the Anglican Church caused much religious ferment. The Cornish may have been particularly sensitive to this issue, since they had already had a foreign faith and form of worship forced upon them.[44] It seemed to many Cornish people that the established church did not care about their spiritual and bodily needs, and:

"The gap between the Anglican Church and the people was still further widened by the identification of the former with a social order and by the transformation of its clergy into a caste of worldly society. Formerly, the church had unified society; all members were equal, at least theoretically, in the presence of the divinity."[45]

At the time of the *Ordinalia* Cornwall had been a participant in a vibrant, pan-European catholic culture, and, though thanks to its natural resources and the ingenuity and hard work of its people, it was playing an important part in the emerging new world of the Industrial Revolution, it had no independent voice of its own and the price was high.

---

43 Deane, Tony and Tony Shaw (2003). *Folklore of Cornwall*. Stroud, Tempus, p. 15.

44 See, for instance, Fletcher, Anthony (1968)). *Tudor rebellions*. London, Longmans, Chapter 5; and Deacon, *op. cit.*, Chapter 3 for the Prayer Book Rebellion; and Spriggs, M. "Additional thoughts on the medieval Cornish Bible", in Payton, Philip (ed) (2006). *Cornish Studies* 14; and Grigg, E. "The medieval Cornish Bible: more evidence", in Payton, Philip (ed) (2008). *Cornish Studies* 16, for the continuing debate on the Cornish translation of the Holy Bible, possibly the work of John Trevisa.

45 See Rowe, John, *op. cit.*, pp. 261.1 *et seq.*

On a local level though, the holy wells may have provided a focus for beleaguered communities, as well as meeting the needs of individuals. In west Cornwall for instance, on the first three Sunday mornings in May, children were taken to holy wells, especially that of St Maddern near Penzance, and dipped into the waters to cure them of rickets and other childhood disorders.[46] The well at St Cleer was a "boussening" or ducking-well for the cure of mentally ill people, and so was the well at St Ninne's. St Jesus' well in Miniver was especially famous for the cure of whooping cough.[47] These events must often have been social occasions,[48] and it is interesting that the wells themselves are often associated with symbols of the old faith. At the well at St Cleer, for instance,

> situated not far from the church... considerable remains of the baptistry, which formerly enclosed it, are still standing, and outside, close by, is an old stone cross.[49]

St Ludguan's well was created by the prayers of an Irish saint, and its waters promote good eyesight and eloquence, until the devil destroyed its healing power.[50] In all, of Cornwall's two hundred and twelve listed holy wells, one hundred and eleven are reputed to possess healing qualities.[51]

The sacred significance of the well goes back in time to the myths of the ancient Celts, perhaps even to the Gaulish Apollo who was worshipped before the Celts left their continental home, and in Ireland Connla's well was a source of inspiration and knowledge.[52] But apart from providing a symbol of continuity with the past holy

---

46 See Courtney, Margaret Ann 1998 (1886). *Cornish Feasts and Folklore*. Penzance, Oakmagic Publications, pp. 32–33.

47 Courtney, *op. cit.*, p. 64.

48 The author attended a similar event in Ireland fifty years ago.

49 Courtney, *op. cit.*, p. 61.

50 Hunt, Robert, *op. cit.*, pp. 288–9.

51 Leggat, Peter Ogilvie and Leggat, Denise V. (1987). *The healing wells: Cornish cults and customs*. Redruth, Truran.

52 MacKillop, James (1998). *Dictionary of Celtic mythology*. Oxford, OUP, p. 91.

wells also link Cornwall with other Celtic lands:[53] examples of well-worship are found in Scotland and the Isle of Man for instance.[54] In Brittany holy wells are strongly associated with churches, and with the saints to which the local church has been dedicated, as at the well at St Bieuzy, whose waters are believed to relieve mental illness.[55] In Cornwall too holy wells are associated with saints.

The Saints of Cornwall

Many of the saints after whom Cornish churches are named are ancient, and lived in the period of Christian expansion which followed the collapse of the Roman Empire. Many are obscure, and their historical existence may be doubted.[56] At that time sainthood was by popular acclamation rather than ecclesiastical bureaucracy, and if a man or woman impressed a local community by their spirituality or healing powers then the church upon which the community was centred could be named in their memory. Some of these names may also represent pre-Christian personalities and therefore a form of enduring cultural continuity, and in some ways they did function as guardian spirits; many are associated with holy wells, for instance, Saint Senara at Zennor is associated with the holy well Venton Zennor, and one wonders if her identity may have become blurred with that of the more famous mermaid. Saints often lived by the side of the holy wells named after them, as did St Agnes who also appears on one of Hunt's giant stories, in which she outwits her oversized suitor and preserves her virginity. In fact St Agnes was one of the most famous of Roman martyrs, but the Cornish saint is presumably a different person.

---

53 MacCana, Proinsias 1996. *Celtic Mythology*. London, Chancellor Press, p. 32.

54 Grant, Isabel F. (1961). *Highland folk-ways*. London, Routledge and Kegan Paul, pp. 306–307; Rhys, Sir John 1980 (1901). *Celtic folklore: Welsh and Manx*. London, Wildwood House, pp. 332–3.

55 Spence, Lewis 1997 (no date). *Legends and Romances of Brittany*. New York, Dover, pp. 381–2.

56 For this and what follows, see John, Catherine Rachel (1981). *The Saints of Cornwall*. Redruth, Truran; and Attwater, Donald (1965). *The Penguin Dictionary of Saints*.

We have already seen that many Cornish wells, with whom the saints are strongly associated, possess healing properties. In the late medieval play *Bewnans Meriasek*, "The Life of St Meriasek", we also find miracles of healing, which are of course a commonplace of medieval hagiography:

"Jhesu, Arluth nef ha'n bys,   700
yeghes dheugh-why re wrontyo!
Jhesu, Arluth, my a'th pys
lemmyn saw an keth tus-ma.
Marya, Mam lun a ras,
pys dhe'th Vap Arluth ragtha."   705

"May Jesus, Lord of heaven and earth,
grant you health!
Jesus, Lord, I pray thee
now heal these same men.
Mary, Mother full of grace.
pray to thy Son and Lord for them"[57]

The play was one of a number of Cornish language texts produced at Glasney College at Penryn under the provostship of John Pascoe in the late fifteenth century, at a time when the bishops of Exeter were attempting to replace "Celtic" dedications of Cornish churches with Latin ones. (At Camborne they were trying to replace the old dedication to St Meriadoc himself by that of St Martin.)[58] In that sense, the play may be seen as an assertion of Cornish individuality, and others have seen it as a "subversive document" in the wake of the 1497 rebellion. In this reading the evil King Teudar of the play represents Henry Tudor, or Henry VII, seen by the Cornish as an oppressor.[59]

---

57 Nance, Robert Morton, and A. S. D. Smith, (eds) (1966). *St Meriasek in Cornwall (Bewnans Meriasek)*. The Federation of Old Cornwall Societies, pp. 12–13.

58 Whetter, James (1988). *The History of Glasney College*. Padstow, Tabb House, p. 108.

59 See Philip Payton (1993). "A … concealed envy against the English: a note on the aftermath of the 1497 rebellion in Cornwall", in Payton, Philip (ed), *Cornish*

Until the year 2000 *Bewnans Meriasek* was thought to be the sole surviving saint's play in the Cornish language.[60] But, in that year was discovered the manuscript of *Bewnans Ke*, "The Life of St Kea" among papers bequeathed to the National Library of Wales by Professor J E Caerwyn Williams. Like the *Ordinalia* and *Bewnans Meriasek*, the *Bewnans Ke* seems to have been by one of the secular priests associated with the college of St Thomas the Martyr at Glasney in Penryn, possibly Radulph Ton, who completed the *Meriasek* manuscript. The fragmentary life of Kea tells the story of the saint's travels across the sea, (he floats on a stone, like St Piran and Saint Ia), and his theological debate with Teudar, as a result of which the saint is imprisoned. Kea's sanctity enables him to survive his ordeal. Eventually the king releases Kea and grants him land at Rosewa to build a church. On his way there Kea prays for water and a well miraculously springs up. Kea uses the holy water to cure a leper. When he arrives at Rosewa Christ sends him stags to help plough the land. Teuday sends a messenger to fetch Kea and seeks to be reconciled to him. Kea asks for as much land as he can enclose while Teudar is taking a bath. The bath is prepared by Oubra, a wise woman and a healer. Teudar finds himself stuck in the bath, and his best land is lost. The play goes on to deal with King Arthur's conflict with Lucius Hiberius, Emperor of Rome, and Modred's adultery with Guinevere, a fascinating episode though it does not concern us here. The parish of St Kea, which had links with Glasney possessed two "playing places" or open-air heaths, and the saint's play was probably first performed at one of them.

That the English bishops were trying to replace Cornish dedications with Latin ones suggests that the old saints provided a focus for the national identity which had already provoked two risings and posed a serious challenge to the emerging English nation-

---

Studies: One. Exeter (1993) pp. 4−13; and Kent, Alan M. (2000). *The Literature of Cornwall: continuity, identity, difference 1000−2000*. Bristol, Redcliffe Press, pp. 44−48.

60 For this and what follows, see Thomas, Graham, and Nicholas Williams (eds) (2007). *Bewnans Ke: The life of St Kea*. Exeter, University of Exeter Press. See also Pascoe, W. H. (1985). *Teudar: a king of Cornwall*. Redruth, Truran.

state of the Tudors.[61] Placing the two great healing saints in the Cornish language at the heart of Cornish culture was a defiant affirmation of that culture in the face of violent encroachment from the east. By Hunt's time cultural assimilation was almost complete, and his collection is inspired by the need to gather up the fragments before they are lost. The stories of mermaids too, which had for so long provided a way of speaking about desire and danger, were fading away as the communities which sustained them were bled by emigration, and the violent swings an unregulated early capitalism appeared to leave little space for the imaginative responsiveness which had always been such an important part of the Cornish world-view. But still Cornwall's folklore hints at the possibility of such a space.

---

61 Thomas and Williams, *op. cit.*, pp. xxvii–xxxiv.

Chapter 4

The Lawyer and the King

Tregeagle

The first series of Hunt's famous *Popular Romances of the West of England* contains a selection of stories about John Tregeagle, a distinction accorded to such other topics as "The Giants", "The Fairies", and "The Mermaids", all subjects which most people would consider central to the body of Cornish folklore. Whether this reflects the importance of the stories to the "droll tellers" and the communities which they served is hard to tell.

The historic Jan or John Tregeagle lived in the seventeenth century and belonged to the family which once owned Trevorder near Bodmin. He was a wealthy magistrate who was tyrannical and unjust and abused his position.[1] He was described as a greedy and unscrupulous landlord, a secret murderer who sacrificed his own sisters for money, whose cruelty caused the death of his wife and children. As his death approached the devils gathered together to seize his soul, and he turned to the priests to save himself. By exorcism they drove the demons away, and Tregeagle was buried with his ancestors in St Breock church.

Then a dispute concerning the ownership of land broke out between two local families. The deceased Tregeagle had acted as steward to one of the claimants and had falsified documents to make it look as if he himself was the land's real owner. He then sold and leased some of this illegally acquired land and kept the money. After his death his criminal proceedings came to light.[2] The case

---

1   For this and what follows see Hunt, Robert (IPPI 3rd Edition). *Popular Romances of the West of England*. London, Chatto and Windus, pp. 132–146.

2   Hunt, Robert, *op. cit.*, p. 133.

eventually came to court, and the judge was about to sum up when the defendant called one final witness, Tregeagle himself who, in another version, comments ominously

"it will not be such an easy task to get rid of me as it has been to call me!"[3]

The dead Tregeagle gave his evidence, and disclosed his frauds, and as a result the defendant won his case. But after the trial Tregeagle remained, while the good and bad angels fought over his soul. The defendant was ordered to remove his witness, but replied:

"To bring him from the grave has been to me so dreadful a task that I leave him to your care, and that of the Prior, by whom he was so beloved."[4]

Treageagle's Tasks

So clergy were summoned, and they decided to give him at least a chance of salvation by setting him a task which would keep the demons at bay but which was so difficult that it would take the whole of eternity to complete it: it was thought that this might allow him to repent of his sins and be saved. The task was to empty Dozmary, or Dozmare pool, which was supposed to be bottomless, using only a limpet shell with a hole in it.

For years Tregeagle worked at his impossible task, but the water grew no lower and Satan continued to watch, hoping for a chance at seizing his soul. Eventually the Evil One caused a terrific thunder storm, and Tregeagle fled, pursued by demons. Tregeagle doubled back to the lake, but the devils caught him up before he could resume his task. Then he ran over the pool and escaped his pursuers (since demons, like witches, cannot cross water), and ran to the chapel on Roach Rock, sticking his head through the window and so claiming sanctuary.

The Hermit of the Rock prayed to be free of his terrible visitor. Each prayer was torture to the ears of the damned Tregeagle, and

---

3   Deane, Tony and Tony Shaw (2003). *Folklore of Cornwall*. Stroud, Tempus, p. 83.

4   Hunt, Robert, *op. cit.*, p. 134.

he roared and shrieked as the devils outside waited to seize him the moment he withdrew his head from the protection of the church. The noise was so unbearable that the rock became deserted, and the saint of the rock was wasting away. The situation became so bad that the monks and priests of Bodmin met together and decided to send Tregeagle, under the protection of two saints, to the north coast near Padstow, and employ him in making trusses of sand and ropes of sand with which to bind them. But every time Tregeagle formed his trusses of sand on the beach, the waves came and washed them away. Every night the howling of the tormented man kept the people of Padstow awake.

In response to their prayers Saint Petroc chained Tregeagle and led him away to Bareppa near Helston on the south coast, and told him to carry sacks of sand across the estuary to Porthleven, knowing that the tide would carry the sand back again.

Though his struggles were "giant like", Tregeagle's task was once again impossible, and once again his shrieks of despair disturbed the rest of the local inhabitants. One of the devils tripped him up as he was carrying a huge sack of sand, and he dropped the sack as he fell, creating the sandbar which still blocks the harbour. The priests once more placed him in chains and sent him to Lands End to sweep the sands from Porthcurnow around the headland into Nanjisal Cove, against the current, "a task which must endure until the world shall end." And:

> even until today is Tregeagle labouring at his task. In calms his wailing is heard; and those sounds which some call the "coughing of the wind" are known to be the moanings of Tregeagle, while the coming storms are predicated by the fearful roarings of this condemned mortal.[5]

This is the core of Tregeagle's story, and variants of it are found all over Cornwall, some of which are recorded by Hunt. One account from "a much esteemed correspondent" provides some interesting detail and variations.[6] In his version, Tregeagle was a steward to Lord

---

5   Hunt, Robert, *op. cit.*, p. 138.

6   Hunt, Robert, *op. cit.*, p. 139 et seq.

C. (like Tom in "The Mermaid's Vengeance") and one can see why Cornish people might be sensitive to the issues of land ownership and fraud. Though enclosure was less of an issue in the Duchy than it was in more easterly counties, smallholdings were being merged into larger farms from the late eighteenth century on, causing a drift of people away from the land which contributed to the huge rise in emigration which continued on into the twentieth century.[7]

In this version the minister drew a circle on the floor and called out three times: "Jahn Tergagle, Jahn Tergagle, Jahn Tergagle", and, "I've heerd the ould men tell it". Tregeagle stood before him in the circle. After the trial,

> "Tergagle he gave men a great deal of trouble, he was knackin' about the place, and wouldn't lave men alone at all."[8]

The people asked the minister to exorcize the ghost. Initially he refused, but eventually he agreed to do it in return for three hundred pounds. First, he bound the troubled spirit to the "epping stock", (a stone step for mounting horses) at Churchtown, then to the "ould oven" at Tevurder, and, in a nice detail, "James Wyatt down to Wadebridge, he was there when they did open it", and finally he was bound to Dozmary pool, where he is still, trying to empty the pool with a limpet shell.[9]

Other accounts render the story as a Faustian parable, and allege that Tregeagle sold his soul to the Devil.[10] According to Deane and Shaw, Tregeagle's soul flaps around Lands End like a huge gull or alternatively haunts Bodmin Moor as a giant bird luring travellers to their deaths. He also pursued the debtor in the trial at which he appeared in the shape of a black bull.[11] Hunt's reference to his "giant

7 Rowe, John (1953). *Cornwall in the Age of the Industrial Revolution*. St Austell, Cornish Hillside Publications, p. ix.

8 Hunt, Robert, *op. cit.*, p. 140.

9 Hunt, Robert, *op. cit.*, p. 140.

10 See, for instance, Westwood, Jennifer, and Jacqueline Simpson (2005). *The Lore of the Land*. London, Penguin.

11 Deane and Shaw, *op. cit.* pp. 83–5.

like struggles", and MacKillop's assertion that he is "sometimes seen as a hostile giant", seem to link the tormented lawyer with the characteristically Cornish body of giant stories,[12] just as his striking connection with water and the sea connect him with the spirits of those places.

Time and Space

Although Tregeagle, unusually for a character in folktale, is identified with a historic seventeenth century character, his association with natural forces such as wind and storm suggest an ancient, elemental character. As Hunt himself says:

> Tregeagle belongs to the mythologies of the oldest nations, and the traditions of this wandering spirit in Cornwall, which centre upon one tyrannical magistrate, are but the appropriation of stories which belong to every age and country.[13]

But in many ways Tregeagle inhabits a medieval world. Good and bad angels compete for his soul, which in some versions is bought by the Devil; he is exorcized by Saint Petroc, from Cornwall's golden age of Celtic Christianity (which links Tregeagle to the other major corpus of Cornish legend, the lives of the saints), and there is a hermit on the rock.

At the same time the law case, the land dispute and the fraud issue seem to place him firmly in a nineteenth-century context. In some respects Tregeagle resembles a romantic hero (Heathcliffe in *Wuthering Heights* also suffers terribly and has some demonic characteristics[14] and the two characters share an association with wild moorland and natural forces). Tregeagle's travels, from Bodmin to Padstow, then to Helston and then Porthcurnow, seem to identify him with the whole of Cornwall, and give him a national significance: in the mid-century economic crisis his character may

---

12 MacKillop, James (1998). *Dictionary of Celtic Mythology*. Oxford, Oxford University Press, p. 364.

13 Hunt, Robert, *op. cit.*, p. 132.

14 A Cornish aunt played a significant role in Emily Brontë's upbringing.

have embodied the trauma of an exhausted and despairing country, as well as the eternal psychological conflict between the impulses of the id and the judgement of the superego or moral sense. Of course Tregeagle's actions are antisocial, and transgress the moral values which hold a small community together, especially in times of crisis. Tregeagle's story reaches deep down into the legendary and historic past, as it speaks to the present and points the way to the future.

Sin and Redemption

And indeed, to eternity, for Tregeagle's task continues to the end of time, and his immortal soul is at stake. A major theme of his story is atonement for sin. As the clergy deliberate on what to do with Tregeagle's troubled spirit, Hunt says:

> They could resign him to the devil at once, but by long trial the worst of crimes might be absolved, and as good churchmen they could not sacrifice a human soul. The only thing was to give the spirit some task, difficult beyond the power of human nature, which might be extended far into eternity. Time might then soften the obdurate soul, which still retained all the black dyes of the sins done in the flesh, that, by infinitely slow degrees repentance might exert its softening power.[15]

Though his punishment is terrible, it is not so hopeless as it appears, for by atoning for his sins he may in the end be saved. Atonement of course lies at the heart of the Christian faith. By his suffering on the cross Christ atones for our sins and saves our souls from damnation. This theme was the main preocccupation of middle Cornish literature. In the great trilogy the *Ordinalia*, for instance, the second play is devoted to Christ's Passion, and dominated by the idea that Christ suffers to redeem the human race from sin. After the crucifixion, which seems to be set in Cornwall, Nicodemus says:

---

15 Hunt, Robert, *op. cit.*, p. 134.

"Gosloweugh oll, A dus vas: 3217
bennath Jhesu, lun a ras,
dheugh kefrys gour ha benen!
Fatel vu Cryst mertherys
rak kerensa tus an bys
why a welas yn tyen."   3222

"Hearken all, O good people:
the blessing of Jesus, full of grace,
to you both man and woman!
How Christ was martyred
for the sake of the people of the world
you have wholly seen."[16]

The fifteenth century poem *Pascon agan Arluth* also centres on
Christ's suffering and its redemptive power.

Warlyrgh mab den ʒe begha / reson prag y fe prynnys   50
yw ihesus crist ʒe ordna / yn neff y vonas tregys
y vos kyllys ny vynna / y doull ganso o tewlys
rag henna ʒe bob dyʒgthtya / forth a rug ʒe vos sylwys.   56

After mankind had sinned, the reason that he was redeemed
is that Jesus Christ decreed that he should dwell in heaven.
He did not intend that man be lost; his plan he had
      determined.
Therefore he provided a way through which all men could
      be saved.[17]

Of course Tregeagle is guilty and suffers for the sins he has himself
committed, while Christ is innocent and suffers for the sins of others,
but nonetheless his story embodies the possibility of redemption, a
theme which links up with the wider European tradition and

---

16 This modern Cornish version is from Nance, Robert Morton and Smith, A. S.
    D. (eds) (1982). *The Cornish Ordinalia; Second Play: Christ's Passion*. Kesva an Tavas
    Kernewek.
17 Williams, Nicholas, Michael Everson, and Alan M. Kent (2020). *The Charter Frag-
    ment and Pascon agan Arluth*. (Corpus Textuum Cornicorum; 1). Dundee: Evertype.

Cornwall's own literary and religious past. On his travels he embraces the whole of Cornwall, and in the mid-nineteenth century crisis it may be that his story was experienced as a response to the new "peripheralism", a response which took its audience back beyond the first peripheralism which descended after the Prayer Book Rebellion, to a time when Cornwall was still its historic self, and part of a wider world.

Bodmin

The historic Tregeagle came from Trevorder near Bodmin and was said to have been buried at St Breock, a large moorland village south of Wadebridge, where Cornish plays were apparently performed in the late middle ages.[18] Tregeagle is also associated with the Midnight Hunter and his "wish hounds" which seem to be a Cornish variant of the widespread Wild Hunt, a ghostly huntsman and his phantom dogs, who are seen, or more usually heard galloping across the sky at night. Sightings are also common in Devon, where the wish hounds are to be found on the Abbot's Way, "an ancient road which extends into Cornwall" and elsewhere.[19] They were often thought to be "demons pursuing dead sinners",[20] which may explain the link with Tregeagle. In John Penwarne's ballad, "Tregeagle or Dozmare Poole: An Anciente Cornishe legende, in two parts",[21] Tregeagle is a shepherd who sells his soul to the Devil, and kidnaps the Earl of Cornwall's daughter. In the end the lady is rescued, and Tregeagle is pursued by the "Black Hunter" and his hounds, as he is to this day.

Dozmare Pool itself was once thought to be bottomless, and such places in Celtic myth are doorways to the Otherworld.[22] They certainly retained a numinous atmosphere into the Christian era and often attracted votive objects in large numbers, as at Llyn Cerrig Bach for instance.[23]

18 Bakere, Jane (1980). *The Cornish Ordinalia*. Cardydd University of Wales Press.
19 Simpson and Roud, *op. cit.*, p. 390
20 Hunt, Robert, *op. cit.*, p. 145.
21 Hunt, Robert, *op. cit.*, p. 143.
22 MacKillop, *op. cit.*, p. 317.
23 MacKillop, *op. cit.*, p. 266. See also Lynch, Frances (1970). *Prehistoric Anglesey*. Anglesey, pp. 249–77.

On Bodmin Moor itself "the most terrifying thing ever to happen" was the appearance of the spirit of King William Rufus, who was murdered in the New Forest by Walter Tyrell in the year 1100.[24] The Norman Robert Earl of Moreton was appointed Earl of Cornwall by William the Conqueror, and seized the priory of St Petroc and its lands at Bodmin. Hunting on the moors one day he saw a large black goat carrying the black figure of William Rufus on its back, naked and pierced through the breast, (the king had been shot with an arrow). When Robert confronted the beast it replied, "I am carrying your king to judgement". It further revealed itself as an evil spirit, sent by St Alban to punish William Rufus for his oppression of the Church. This incident, it later transpired, occurred at the exact time when the king had been killed in the New Forest. This story is one of a number told by monastic chroniclers who resented William's policies, but it must have had a particular resonance in Cornwall, with its themes of foreign oppression, land theft (which also occurs in the tale of Tregeagle) and religious persecution. Tregeagle is also associated with supernatural and demonic animals.

King Arthur

But Bodmin Moor is also associated with memories of a very different king. Sites on the moor include King Arthur's Hall and King Arthur's Downs, King Arthur's Bed near Twelve Men's Moor, and King Arthur's Quoit, a name which recalls several giant-inspired placenames.[25]

The cultural life of King Arthur is a long and complicated one, and is by no means over. Since the narrative has been distorted by many film adaptations over the last twenty years, it might be best to begin with a brief summary of what is actually known.[26]

---

24 Westwood and Simpson, *op. cit.*, p. 89

25 See Seddon, Richard (1990). *The Mystery of Arthur at Tintagel*. London, Rudolf Steiner Press.

26 For this and what follows see Alcock, Leslie (1971). *Arthur's Britain*. London, Allen Lane. Loomis, Roger Sherman (ed) (1959). *Arthurian Literature in the Middle Ages*. Oxford, Clarendon Press. Hale, Amy, Alan M. Kent, and Tim Saunders (eds) (2000). *Inside Merlin's Cave: A Cornish Arthurian Reader 1000–2000 AD*.

The historic Arthur, if indeed there was one, was a "dux bellorum" or war leader who led the British resistance to the Saxon invaders in the fifth and sixth centuries. He won a series of twelve battles, culminating at Mount Badon, which halted the Saxon advance for fifty years. He died at the Battle of Camlan, which may have been sited on the Camel River in Cornwall, and which is supposed to have taken place in 538. Such is the bare and questionable outline of history.

The legendary life of Arthur began with Geoffrey of Monmouth's *History of the Kings of Britain*, which tells the story of how Arthur's father Uther Pendragon made love to Ygaerne, wife of Gorlois of Cornwall, with the magic help of Merlin, as a result of which Arthur was conceived. Arthur became king at age 15 and made many conquests, eventually declaring war on Rome (on his way there he kills the giant of St Michael's Mount). In his absence, his nephew, (in some accounts his son) Modred, seizes his wife and the kingdom of Britain. The true king returns and Modred flees to Cornwall, where he dies in a final confrontation. Arthur is carried to the Isle of Avalon to heal his grievous wounds.

This basic legend was extended and embroidered by later English, French and German writers such as Wace, who introduced the Round Table, Layamon, Chretien de Troyes, Marie de France and others. In this way, other characters such as Tristram, Merlin and Lancelot became part of Arthur's story. In this process Arthur was transformed from an obscure guerrilla leader into the epitome of knightly chivalry, the embodiment of the values of the new European ruling order. This vision was expressed magnificently in Sir Thomas Malory's English prose classic *Le Morte d'Arthur* which inspired a host of imitative works down to the present; and most importantly Alfred Lord Tennyson's *Idylls of the King*. This series of twelve connected poems presents the story of Arthur from his meeting with Guinevere to his death at Camlan, and focuses on the adultery of Launcelot and Guinevere. It had a huge impact on Victorian England and inspired great artists such as Edward Burne-Jones. This new Arthur was enlisted into the imperial project, and became a symbol of British supremacy.[27] Stories about him chimed with the new Gothic

---

27 Barczewski, Stephanie L (2000). *Myth and National Identity in Nineteenth-Century Britain*. Oxford, OUP.

style, the public face of Victorian England,[28] which in its growing disillusionment and self-alienation, was beginning to idealize and reconstruct its medieval past.[29]

All this of course had nothing to do with memories of a Celtic resistance leader who was waiting until his people's need should awaken him, traces of which still lingered in Wales, Brittany, and Cornwall.

King Arthur in Cornwall

In Cornwall the new mythos was superimposed on the old, in the service of the fledgling tourist industry. The re-publication of Malory's *Morte d'Arthur* in the early nineteenth century had renewed interest in the Cornish king,[30] and after the railways were introduced later in the century the Arthurian sites became a major tourist attraction. (This was the reason for the almost entirely specious Arthurian connection with Tintagel.) In Tennyson Arthur is strongly associated with the sea and this too fitted well with the new romantic construct of Cornwall as a tourist destination. It was later to play a role in GWR's creation of the "Cornish Riviera".[31] As Mais wrote:

"Old England is everywhere crumbling about our ears, and it is a sorry business trying to find any traces of her nowadays in the Home Counties, but in the Duchy medievalism still exists, the candle lit by the early saints still burns, the age of chivalry is emphatically not dead, and our most remote ancestors still haunt the ancient places."

---

28 See, for instance, Curl, James Stevens (1990). *Victorian Architecture*. Newton Abbot, David and Charles. And Hill, Rosemary (2007). *God's Architect: Pugin and the Building of Romantic Britain*. London, Allen Lane.

29 For a late example of this kind of thing see Stevens, Frank Leonard (1928). *Through Merrie England: The Pageantry and Pastimes of the Village and the Town*. London, Frederick Warne.

30 See Kent, Alan M. (2000). "King Arthur and Literature in Cornwall". In Hale, Kent, and Saunders *op. cit.*, p. 17.

31 Mais, S P B (1928). *The Cornish Riviera*. GWR. Quoted in Thomas, C. (1997). *See your own Country First: The Geography of a Railway Landscape*. In Westland, Ella (1997). *Cornwall: The Cultural Construction of Place*. Penzance, Patten Press, p. 121.

But throughout the Middle Ages, when Arthur became the dominant figure in European literature, Cornwall's memory of its Cornish king had lingered on. It may be that Bodmin was a centre of Arthurian devotion: according to Herman of Laon nine canons from that city visited England in 1113 to raise money. On their approach to Bodmin they were shown Arthur's Chair and Oven. At Bodmin their portable shrine to the Virgin was placed in the church, where it was guarded by a Cornishman with a withered arm. During the night he got into an argument with one of the Frenchmen, who had denied that Arthur still lived, and a near-riot ensued. The belief in Arthur's return clearly embodied national aspirations in Cornwall, and it may be that Bodmin was a focus for such aspirations and the memories that feed them. Of course, such beliefs can also be seen as compensation, a psychological adaptation to the reality of defeat. The story continued to be added to up to the nineteenth century, when the identification of Dozmare Pool with the resting place of Arthur's sword seems to have originated. Of course, such beliefs are of some significance, even when they are recent.

For many years it was believed that there was no Arthurian literature in the Cornish language. But not the least startling outcome of the recovery of *Bewnans Ke*, "The Life of St Kea", the manuscript of a thitherto unknown play in Cornish in the year 2000, was the discovery that it contained Arthurian material. Some of this deals with the seduction of Guinevere and the conflict between Arthur and Modred, which eventually led to the king's death at Camlann, which is known from other sources,[32] and some with the quarrel between Arthur and the emperor Lucius Hiberius, who attempts to levy tribute from Britain: a missing folio apparently dealt with the failure of Ke's attempt to reconcile Arthur and Modred and the saint's return to Brittany. The Arthur of the play is no guerrilla leader, and his story has clearly been influenced by the wider European tradition. At the same time he is a mighty king who receives tribute from other kings and speaks to emperors as an equal.

---

32 Thomas, Graham and Nicholas Williams (eds) (2007). *Bewnans Ke*. Exeter, University of Exeter Press.

(y'n gylwyr Arthur Cornow)   1658

he is called Arthur the Cornishman[33]

Though the play seems to have been written in the middle of the fifteenth century the manuscript dates from the middle or second half of the sixteenth century. The Cornish Rebellion of 1497 led by Thomas Flamank and Michael An Gof was provoked by what were seen as unjust tax levies to support England's war with Scotland. The Cornish army was defeated at Blackheath, and Flamank and An Gof were hung, drawn and quartered. King Henry cancelled an order that their remains should be exhibited throughout Cornwall because of fears that the Duchy was "still eager to promote a revolution if they were in any way provoked".[34]

In this historical context, the defiance (in Cornish) of a Cornish king to a foreign emperor must have had a powerful emotional impact:

"Lavar the'th arluth, cosyn: 2112
me re leverys heb flows
rag an tribut a wovyn
na goyth nahen war nebas ous
the'n stat a Rome
mars e ben ef dyhynnys."   2117

"Tell your lord, my friend:
I have said without trifling
as for the tribute he demands
there does not fall for some time now
to the state of Rome
anything other than his decapitated head."[35]

Other plays were written in Cornish at Glasney College, which seems to have been a centre of Cornish culture until shut down, along with other Cornish institutions, by Henry VIII At the English

---

33 Thomas and Williams. *op. cit.*, p. 171.

34 Fletcher, Anthony (1968). *Tudor Rebellions*. London, Longmans, Green and Co.

35 Thomas and Williams, *op. cit.*, p. 213.

Reformation. The other surviving saint's play, *Bewnans Meriasek*, "The Life of Meriasek", was also written at Glasney. Philip Payton has argued that *Meriasek* may reflect Cornish national feeling in the aftermath of the 1497 rising, and that it is "a subversive document".[36]

Both *Bewnans Ke* and *Bewnans Meriasek* contain dialogue between the saint and a pagan ruler called Teudar, who embodies religious oppression. In *Bewnans Ke* the pagan king says:

> "Out, out, out! I am ful wod.   256
> Harow, harow!
> By Mahumy's precyus blod!
> bethyth marow
> a wel the'n pow.
> Te a levar, tavas pan
> na'th uesta Du saw onyn
> me a bref genas bos gow."   263

> "Out! out! out! I am quite mad
> Alas, alas!
> By Mahound's precious blood!
> You shall die
> in the view of the country.
> You say, you cloth-tongue,
> that you have but one God
> I shall prove that you tell a lie!"[37]

The fact that Muslims are, of course, monotheists was not widely understood in medieval Europe, but the similarity between the names "Teudar" and "Tudor" would not have escaped a Cornish audience, connected as they were by the theme of religious oppression. The fact that Teudar's outburst is in English may also

---

36 Payton, Phillip (1993). "A concealed envy against the English: a note on the aftermath of the 1497 Rebellion in Cornwall". In Payton, Phillip (ed) (1993). *Cornish Studies*: One. See also Kent, Alan M. (2000). *The Literature of Cornwall: Continuity, Identity, Difference*. Bristol, Redcliffe Press, pp. 44–49.

37 Thomas and Williams, *op. cit.*, p. 27.

be relevant. When the English prayer-book was introduced into Cornwall in 1549 it was denounced as

> like a Christmas game... And so we the Cornish men (whereof certain of us understand no English), utterly refuse this new English.

The contempt in this sentence crackles across the centuries. The Cornish rose again, were again defeated, and paid a terrible price.[38] By some counts over half of Cornwall's able-bodied men were murdered by Kingston's troops: villages burned, priests swung from their own bell-ropes, and there is some evidence that Cornish-speaking communities were singled out for special treatment.[39] The language never recovered, and the quantity of folklore lost with the old language must have been enormous.[40]

As for the Cornish plays more generally, they recall a time when Cornwall played a significant role in Catholic European culture, a culture once symbolized by Arthur himself. Brian Murdoch has pointed out that the themes of these plays, the conversion of unbelievers, the relations between church and state, healing and the emphasis on saints and especially the Blessed Virgin, fit closely into the prevalent dramatic model in Europe.[41] The centralizing Tudor nation-state split Cornwall off from Europe and from its past, imposing an alien religion and language. Though the Cornish sense of identity did not disappear—it resurfaced during the Civil War for instance[42]—it was to be more than two hundred years until Cornwall found a new identity as a dynamic industrial region.

38 Payton, Phillip (2004). *Cornwall: A History*. Fowey, Cornwall Editions, p. 123.
39 See Rowse, A. L. (1941). *Tudor Cornwall*. London, Jonathan Cape, pp. 253–290. And Angarrack, John (1999). *Breaking the Chains*. Cambourne, Stannary Publications Passim.
40 See Nance, Robert Morton (1924). *Folk-Lore Recorded in the Cornish Language*. Falmouth, Royal Cornwall Polytechnic. 91st Annual Report.
41 Murdoch, Brian (1993). *Cornish Literature*. Cambridge, Boydell and Brewer, p. 102.
42 See Stoyle, Mark (2005). *Soldiers and Strangers: An Ethnic History of the English Civil War*. New Haven, Yale University Press. And Stoyle, Mark (2002). *West Britons:*

Cornwall in Crisis

Many people today, and in Victorian times, went to Cornwall in search of rural tranquility, but it is important to remember that, in Philip Payton's words:

> The Cornish economy was one of the very first in the world to industrialise, the early and successful application of steam power facilitating the development of deep mining and achieving for Cornwall an envied place in the forefront of technological innovation.[43]

A host of Cornish engineers and inventors, men such as Richard Trevithick and Humphrey Davy, made the new industrial age possible and Cornish beam engines were to be found all over the world. This was accompanied by a wave of scholarly and artistic creativity such as Cornwall had never seen before, as the work of Davies Gilbert, John Opie and William Borlase still testifies. The growth of the tin and copper mining industries in which Cornwall was briefly the world's dominant producer was accompanied by rapid development of the steam engine and locomotive, which was to make a huge contribution to the emerging tourist industry.

But by the time Hunt's *Popular Romances* appeared (itself perhaps one of the last expressions of the Cornish renaissance), the writing was already on the wall. The mines were growing deeper and more expensive to run,[44] and the emergence of competition from the United States, Chile, Cuba and south Australia, where costs were lower, led to the collapse of copper, and the decline of tin, which in turn caused emigration on a huge scale, and the crisis which led to a "second Peripheralism" later in the century.

Cornish Identities and the Early Modern British State. Exeter, University of Exeter Press.

43 Payton, *op. cit.*, p. 180.

44 Payton, Phillip (1992). *The Making of Modern Cornwall: Historical Experience and the Persistence of Difference*. Redruth, Dyllansow Truran, pp. 99–118.

Lost cities

Hunt also refers to traditional stories about lost cities off the Cornish coast. Such stories are not uncommon elsewhere, especially in the Celtic world; one thinks of the Breton city of Ys, and the ringing of its submerged bells, and similar stories are told of Lough Neagh and Cardigan Bay.[45] Such stories may go back to the Celtic Otherworld in one of its aspects, Tir fo Thuinn, "Land under wave", known also in Gaelic Scotland as An t-Eilean Uaine or "the Green Island". The Cornish variants of the submerged city are found at Langarrow, said to have been a beautiful city now buried under sand dunes near Perranporth as a punishment for the greed and dissoluteness of the inhabitants and the more famous Lyonesse (if it is not indeed the same story) in Mount's Bay, where Tennyson placed his Camelot:

> in the lost land of Lyonesse, where, save the Isles of Scilly, all is now wild sea.

As the story goes, Lyonesse was a rich country possessing splendid cities and one hundred and forty churches. One night in 1099 the sea covered it, leaving only the western mountain, the present Isles of Scilly. A man called Trevilian escaped and rode to high ground of Perranuthnoe, and the Trevelyan arms still depict a horse emerging from the sea.[46] And Tresillern on Bodmin Moor is also said to be the site of an inundated settlement.

There are some Arthurian associations with Mount's Bay—Hunt says Arthur defeated the giants there, and that Merlin foretold the Spanish raid of 1595 from a rock near Mousehole. But Lyonesse is most strongly associated with the story of Tristan, his uncle King Mark of Cornwall, and his lover Yseult, the king's wife.

Tristan and Iseult

This triangular love story was hugely popular in medieval Europe, and had several parallels in the Celtic world (the stories of Fionn, Diarmuid and Gráinne, Deirdre and the sons of Uisne, Arthur,

---

45 See Spence, Lewis (1997). *Legends and Romances of Britanny*. New York, Dover, pp. 184–188.

46 Deane and Shaw, *op. cit.*, p. 125.

Lancelot and Guinevere, for instance).[47] All these stories are characterized by conflicting loyalties and a tragic outcome.[48] The story is thus a link between Cornwall and the other Celtic countries, as well as being Cornwall's major contribution to European and indeed world literature.

Many placenames in the story are still to be found in Cornwall,[49] and a granite pillar by the road between Fowey and Par bears the inscription

"Drustans hic lacit Cunomori filius"
"Here lies Drustans son of Cunomorus"

Cunomorus is Mark's name, and Drustans an alternative form of Tristan. Leland's sixteenth century chronicle records a now vanished line on the stone:

"Cum domina Clusilla"
"With a lady called Clusilla"

which could stand for Iseult the Fair. The stone was originally found at Castle Dore, often regarded as Mark's stronghold, and there are other suggestive local names. Possibly some saints names (Geraint, Kea and Just for instance) may refer back to Arthurian characters, and "Morgan Le Fay" may originate in Cornish "Morgan", meaning "sea woman",[50] perhaps "mermaid".[51]

The story received a number of treatments during the Middle Ages. In the twelfth century Welsh Triads he is given what appears to be a pictish name, but it seems to have been Thomas of Britain in

---

47 See McMahon, Brendan (2006). *The Princess who Ate People*. Wymeswold, Heart of Albion Press.

48 The tale of Blodeuwed, Lle Llaw Gyffes, and Gronur Bebyr, Lord of Penllyn is a close Welsh parallel, in the Fourth Branch of the Mabinogi. See Jones, Gwyn and Thomas Jones (1949). *The Mabinogian*, pp. 55–79. It has been brilliantly retold in a contemporary setting by Alan Garner in "The Owl Service".

49 See Padel, Oliver J. (1981). "The Cornish Background of the Tristan Stories". Cambridge, *Medieval Celtic Studies* 1, pp. 53–81.

50 Deane and Shaw, *op. cit.*, pp. 123–131.

51 MacKillop, *op. cit.*, p. 365.

his verse "Tristan" who first placed the lovers in an Arthurian setting, though their love story seems to antedate the Arthurian "Matter of Britain" by some considerable time. Later versions by Gottfried von Strassburg and Beroul shaped the story as we now know it, which is as follows:

Tristan is sent to Ireland to bring back his uncle's betrothed, the Irish Princess Iseult. Iseult's mother prepares a love potion to help her daughter feel some attraction for the ageing King Mark of Cornwall, her future husband. On their voyage Tristan and Iseult drink the potion by mistake and make love, so violating their pledges to the king. After various complications Iseult completes her journey to Cornwall and Tristan goes into exile in Brittany, where he marries Iseult of the White Hands. As he lies mortally wounded his Breton wife tells him that the true Iseult is not on board a ship he is expecting and he dies in despair. Of course this tale is a sophisticated literary artefact, which did not exist in this form in medieval Cornwall. But across medieval Europe the story achieved huge popularity as the epitome of courtly love, the new aristocratic sensibility which dominated continental culture for centuries.

But the story also has a layer which is deeper, older, darker. Reading it now most people will sympathize with the young lovers, but the original story was much more complex. Tristan owed loyalty to his uncle Mark (who, if the Tristan stone is right, was in fact his father), entailing a double obligation. Mark had obligations to Tristan, as his man and kinsman. In neither ancient Cornwall nor medieval Europe would Iseult's role be seen from a feminist perspective, but it is hard not to sympathize: no-one asks her if she actually wants to marry the elderly Cornish king. All people in this story suffer, and it is hard to see how it could be otherwise, or how anyone is really to blame. One imagines that in its original context Iseult would be considered guilty though few modern readers will take that view. Certainly, in ancient Celtic society the role of the woman was to offer the mead-cup, to weave peace and effect reconciliation.[52] The Cornish Arthur is likewise trapped in triadic

52 Enright, Michael J. (1996). *Lady with a Mead Cup: Ritual, Prophecy and Lordship in the European Warzone from La Tene to the Viking Age*. Dublin, 4 Courts Press. Passim.

conflict, as his nephew Modred seduces his wife, and even in the later chivalric variant in which Lancelot and Guinevere betray him in their adulterous relationship. In the later literary versions these relationships are romanticized and something of their emotional immediacy is lost, but the Irish stories of Diarmuid and Gráinne and Deirdre and Fionn retain all their original impact, and can help us understand the original meanings of the Tristan story, which have become fragmented over time, and yet which clearly stem from the same original mindset.

In all these stories a young man who owes allegiance to his lord falls in love with a young woman who is destined to be his lord's wife. Sometimes the woman takes the initiative. Noisiu in the Irish story is wary of Deirdre, until

> she rushed at him and caught the two ears of his head. "Two ears of shame and mockery," she said, "if you do not take me with you." "Woman, leave me alone!" he said. "You will do it," she said, binding him.[53]

It would be too easy to see in these tragic conflicts a vindication of Freud's famous Oedipus theory, which depends on the idea of the son's desire to supplant the father. In Freud's view this "family romance" is the origin of all psychosexual development:

> A single idea of general valued dawned on me. I have found, in my own case too, the phenomena of being in love with my mother and jealous of my father and I now consider it a universal event in early childhood… If this is so, we can understand the gripping power of Oedipus Rex, in spite of all the objections that reason raises against the presupposition of fate… the Greek legend seizes upon a compulsion which everyone recognizes because he senses its existence within himself. Everyone in the audience was once a budding Oedipus in fantasy and each recoils in horror from the dream fulfilment here transplanted into reality, with the full

---

53 Kinsella, Thomas (1970). *The Táin*. Oxford, OUP/Dolmen, p. 12.

quantity of repression which separates his infantile state from his present one.[54]

Of course this begs several questions. If Freud detects this fantasy "in his own case too", how can we be sure that it is not precisely that, his personal fantasy, rather than "a universal event in early childhood"? In any case the Celtic triads while they recall Oedipus, casting the king as the symbolic father, do not exactly mimic it.[55] Nonetheless Freud is surely right to assert the importance of early relationships in human development, in all their joys and sorrows, and the power of ancient stories to express them.[56] While no old Cornish version of Tristan and Iseult has yet been found, and there is some evidence that favours a northern origin, Tristan's association with Lyonesse seems real enough, and history provides a real Mark and a real Tristan in the Arthurian period at Castle Dore, the Iron Age hillfort at St Sampson.[57] The Cornish story is believed to originate in the Irish tale of "Diarmuid and Gráinne", which represents an older, less idealistic tradition, and which openly confronts the tensions and ambiguities of passion. That this was once part of the Cornish tradition, before it fed into medieval romance, can scarcely be doubted.

A distinctively Cornish story, though it apparently goes back to the Gospel of Nicodemus, "The Legend of the Rood" appears in the *Ordinalia* plays. Halliday summarizes it thus:

God exiles Adam from his face until such time as he shall choose to grant him the oil of mercy. When Adam is more than nine hundred years old and infirm, he sends his son

---

54 Masson, Jeffrey M. (1985). *The Complete Letters of Sigmund Freud to Wilhelm Fliess 1887–1904*. Cambridge, Harvard University Press, p. 272.

55 The female characters are much less passive, and there is more emphasis on the persecutory "Oedipal father".

56 See McMahon, Brendan (1998). "Triadic Relationships in Celtic Traditional Narrative: The Limitations of Applied Psychoanalysis". *British Journal of Psychotherapy*. 15: 1, Autumn 1998, pp. 90–99.

57 Westwood, Jennifer (1987). *Albion: A Guide to Legendary Britain*. London, Paladin, pp. 10–12.

Seth to Paradise, along the path trodden by him and Eve
when they were expelled, to ask the angel if he shall have the
oil of mercy before he dies. The angel tells Seth to look
within the gate, and there he sees a fair country, a spring and
four streams, and a great tree with bare branches, withered
and dry like the prints of Adam's feet. He looks again, and
sees an adder in the tree, but when he looks a third time, he
sees a new-born child crying in the top, which reaches into
the sky, and Abel, the first man to suffer death, lying at the
roots in Hell. The angel explains that the child is Christ, who
will cleanse Adam's sin: he is the oil of mercy. He then gives
him three seeds of the apple tasted by Adam, which placed
under his tongue after his death, shall grow into cedar,
cypress and pine. Seth tells his father, who laughs for joy
before he dies, and is buried in the Vale of Hebron. The
seeds grow into three wands, and all high, which remain
green and are the same size till the time of Moses.

when they come together to form one stem.[58]

The holy tree reappears from time to time throughout sacred
history until it is eventually used to make the cross upon which Christ
was crucified. It was lost, then rediscovered by Helena, mother of
Constantine, the first Christian emperor, who divided it into four
parts, which were placed in the Temple at Rome, Alexandria and
St Sophia's in Constantinople, where it performed many miracles.
Its place is thus at the very centre of the Christian tradition. The
holy rood or cross of course symbolizes the atonement, the
redemption from sin which is a central theme of the Tregeagle story.

Conclusion

For as long as they have existed folk tales have helped people to
negotiate the psychological, sexual and spiritual quandaries which
face them in every generation: in more recent times, literature has
taken on this function. So Tregeagle deals with sin and atonement,
Arthur with death and defeat, Tristan and Iseult with the
contradictions and conflicts which complicate our sad passions. But

---

58 Halliday, F. E. (1955). *The Legend of the Rood*. London, Duckworth, pp. 46–7.

such stories are never static, and they change in response to the changing needs of the communities they serve. So Tregeagle in Hunt may represent Cornwall's crisis, Arthur its reawakening sense of nationhood (the language revivalists self-consciously made use of Arthurian legend in their ritual and literature).[59] Sadly, the forces of cultural and economic change were sweeping away what remained of folk narrative just as Hunt and Bettrell were collecting the fragments and preserving them for future generations.

---

59 See Hale, Kent, and Saunders, *op. cit.*, items 39, 40, 43, 45 for instance.

Bibliography

Alcock, Leslie (1971). *Arthur's Britain*. London, Allen Lane.

Angarrack, John (1999). *Breaking the Chains*. Cambourne, Stannary Publications Passim.

Apuleius (trans. Robert Graves) (1950). *The Golden Ass*. Harmondsworth, Penguin.

Arnold, Matthew (1910) (1867). *On the Study of Celtic Literature and other Essays*. London, J M Dent.

Attwater, Donald (1965). *The Penguin Dictionary of Saints*.

Bakere, Jane (1980). *The Cornish Ordinalia: A Critical Study*. Cardiff, University of Wales Press.

Baldick, Chris (ed.) (1992). *The Oxford Book of Gothic Tales*. Oxford, Oxford University Press.

Barkan, David (1996). *The Duality of Human Existence: Isolation and Communion in Western Man*. New York, Beacon Press.

Barczewski, Stephanie L. (2000). *Myth and National Identity in Nineteenth Century Britain*. Oxford, Oxford University Press.

Berresford Ellis, Peter (1974). *The Cornish Language and its Literature*. London, Routledge and Kegan Paul.

Bettelheim, Bruno (1976). *The Uses of Enchantment: The Meaning and Importance of Fairy Tales*. New York, Alfred A Knopf. Reprint (1978), Harmondsworth, Penguin.

Birch, Lionel (1906). *Stanhope, A., Forbes A. R. A., and Elizabeth Stanhope Forbes, A. R. W. S.* London, Cassell.

Booker, Christopher (2004). *The Seven Basic Plots: Why we Tell Stories*. London, Blooksbury.

Bottrell, William (1870). *Traditions and Hearthside Stories of West Cornwall*. Penzance, the author. Reprint (1996), Lampeter, Llanerch Press.

Bottrell, William (1880). *Stories and Folklore of West Cornwall*. Reprinted (1996), Llanerch.

Bray, Anna Eliza (1844). *Traditions, Legends, Superstitions, and Sketches of Devonshire on the Borders of the Tamar*. 2 vols, London.

Breait, H. (1952). *400 Centuries of Cave Art Montignac*. Centre d'Études et de Documentation Pré-Historiques.

Briggs, Asa (1963). *Victorian Cities*. London, Odhams.

Briggs, Katherine (1967). *The Fairies in Tradition and Literature*. London, Routledge and Kegan Paul.

Briggs, Katherine (1976). *A Dictionary of Fairies*. London, Allen Lane.

Broome, Dora (1963). *Fairy Tales from the Isle of Man*. Douglas, Modern Press.

Campbell, John Francis (1860—61). *Popular Tales of the West Highlands*. 3 vols, Edinburgh, Edmonston and Douglas. Reprint (1983—84), Hounslow, Wildwood House.

Carew, Richard (1602). *Survey of Cornwall*. Reprinted (2000), Redruth, Tamar Books.

Chadorow, Nancy (1978). *The Reproduction of Mothering: Psychoanalysis and the Sociology of Gender*. Berkeley, University of California Press.

Collins, Wilkie (1851). *Rambles Beyond Railways*. London, Richard Bentley. Reprint (1982), London, A Mott.

Collins, Wilkie. *The Moonstone*.

Collins, Wilkie. *The Woman in White*.

Courtney, Margaret Ann (1886). *Cornish Feasts and Folklore*. Reprinted (1998), Oakmagic.

Crossing, William (1890). *Tales of the Dartmoor Pixies: Glimpses of Elfin Haunts and Antics*. London, Hood.

Curl, James Stevens (1990). *Victorian Architecture*. Newton Abbot, David and Charles.

Curtin, Jeremiah (1890). *Myths and Folklore of Ireland*. London, Sampson Low, Marston, Searle and Rivington. Reprint (1975), New York, Gramercy.

Davidson, Hilda Ellis and Anna Chaudhri (eds.) (2003). *A Companion to the Fairy Tale*. Cambridge, D S Brewer.

Deacon, Bernard, Dick Cole, and Garry Tregigda (2003). *Mebyon Kernow and Cornish Nationalism*. Cardiff, Welsh Academic Press.

Deacon, Bernard, (2007). *Cornwall: A Concise History*. Cardiff, University of Wales Press.

Deane, Tony, and Tony Shaw (1975). *The Folklore of Cornwall*. London, Batsford. Reprint (2003), Stroud, Tempus Publishing.

Desmond, Adrian, and James Moore (1991). *Darwin*. London, Michael Joseph.

Dorson, Richard M. (1968). *The British Folklorists*. London, Routledge and Kegan Paul.

Drabble, Margaret (ed) (2000). *Oxford Companion to English Literature*. Oxford, Oxford University Press.

Duffy, Maureen (1972). *The Erotic World of Faery*. London, Hodder and Stoughton.

Dundes, Alan (1984). *Sacred Narrative: Readings in the Theory of Myth*. University of California Press.

Enright, Michael J. (1996). *Lady with a Mead Cup: Ritual, Prophecy and Lordship in the European Warzone from La Tène to the Viking Age*. Dublin, 4 Courts Press Passim.

Evans, Eric J. (1983). *The Forging of the Modern State: Early Industrial Britain, 1783—1870*. London, Pearson.

BIBLIOGRAPHY

Faber, Geoffrey C. (1933). *Oxford Apostles: A Character Study of the Oxford Movement*. London, Faber and Faber. Reprint (1954), Harmondsworth, Penguin Books.

Fletcher, Anthony (1968). *Tudor Rebellions*. London, Longmans.

Ford, Boris (ed) (1992). *Cambridge Cultural History of Britain. Volume 7: Victorian Britain*. Cambridge, Cambridge University Press.

Gay, Peter (1988). *Freud: A Life for our Time*. London, Dent.

Georges, Robert A., and Michael Owen Jones (1995). *Folkloristics: An Introduction*. Bloomington, Indiana University Press.

Gilbert Davies (1826) *Mount Calvary, Interpreted in the English Tongue*. London, Nichols.

Gimbutas, Marija (1989). *The Language of the Goddess*. London, Thames and Hudson.

Glasscock, Carl B. (1938). *The War of the Copper Kings*. New York.

Grant, Isabel F. (1961). *Highland Folk-Ways*. London, Routledge and Kegan Paul.

Green, Miranda (1986). *The Gods of the Celts*.

Grennan, Margaret Rose (1945). *William Morris, Medievalist and Revolutionary*. New York, King's Crown Press.

Griscom, Acton (ed) (1929). *Geoffrey of Monmouth, Historia Regum Britannia*. New York.

Hale, Amy, Alan M. Kent, and Tim Saunders (eds) (2000). *Inside Merlin's Cave: A Cornish Arthurian Reader 1000–2000 AD*.

Halliday, F. E. (1955). *The Legend of the Rood*. London, Duckworth.

Halliday, F. E. (1959). *A History of Cornwall*. London, Gerald Duckworth.

Hamilton Jenkin, Alfred Kenneth (1927). *The Cornish Miner*. London, Allen and Unwin.

Hamilton Jenkin, Alfred Kenneth (1933). *Cornwall and the Cornish: The Story, Religion and Folk-lore of the Western Land*. London, J M Dent.

Harte, Jeremy (2004). *Explore Fairy Traditions*. Loughborough, Heart of Albion.

Hartland, Edwin Sidney (1891). *The Science of Fairy Tales: An Inquiry into Fairy Mythology*. London, Walter Scott.

Heaney, Seamus (2010). *Beowulf: A Verse Translation*. London, Folio.

Hill, Charles Peter (1977). *British Economic and Social History 1700–1975*. London, Edward Arnold.

Hill, Rosemary (2007). *God's Architect: Pugin and the Building of Romantic Britain*. London, Allen Lane.

Hobsbawm, Eric (1962). *The Age of Revolution 1789–1848*. London, Weidenfeld and Nicolson.

Hobsbawm, Eric (1975). *The Age of Capital*. London, Weidenfeld and Nicolson

Hooper, E. G. Retallack (eds) (1985), *Gwryans an Bys or The Creation of the World*. Redruth, Dyllansow Truran.

Howells, William (1831). *Cambrian Superstitions*. London, Longmans. Reprint (1991), Felinfach, Llanerch Press.

Hughes, Winifred (1980). *The Maniac in the Cellar: Sensation Novels of the 1860s.* New Jersey, Princeton University Press.

Hull, Eleanor (1928). *Folklore of the British Isles.* London, Methuen.

Hunt, John Dixon (1982). *The Wider Sea: A Life of John Ruskin.* London, Dent.

Hunt, Robert (1881). *Popular Romances of the West of England.* London, Chatto and Windus.

James, Ronald M. (1992). "Knockers, knackers and ghosts. Immigrant folklore in the western mines". In *Western Folklore*, vol 51, Part 2, 153–177.

Jenkins, A. K. Hamilton (1927). *The Cornish Miner.* London, Allen and Unwin.

Jenkins, A. K. Hamilton (1933). *Cornwall and the Cornish.*

Jenner, Henry (1904). *A Handbook of the Cornish Language.* London, D Nutt. New edition (2010) Cathair na Mart, Evertype.

John, Catherine Rachel (1981). *The Saints of Cornwall.* Redruth, Dyllansow Truran.

Jones, Gwyn, and Thomas Jones (1949). *The Mabinogion.* London, J M Dent.

Jones, Kelvin I. (ed) (1996). *Cornish Fairy Folk.* Penzance, Oakmagic.

Kennedy, Patrick (1891). *Legendary Fictions of the Irish Celts.* London, Macmillan. Reprint (1998), Felinfach, Llanerch Press.

Kent, Alan M. (2000). *The Literature of Cornwall: Continuity, Identity, Difference, 1000–2000.* Bristol, Redcliffe Press.

Kinsella, Thomas (1970). *The Táin.* Oxford, Oxford University Press/Dolmen.

Kristeva, Julia (1989). *Black Sun.* New York, Columbia University Press.

Laming, Annette (1959). *Lascaux. Paintings and Engravings.* Harmondsworth, Penguin.

Laplanche, Jean, and Jean-Bertrand Pontalis (1988). *The Language of Psychoanalysis.* London, Karnac Books and the Institute of Psychoanalysis.

Leggat, Peter Ogilvie, and Denise V. Leggat (1987). *The Healing Wells: Cornish Cults and Customs.* Redruth, Truran

Lönnrot, Elias (1989). *The Kalevala.* Trans Keith Bosley. Oxford, Oxford University Press.

Loomis, Roger Sherman (ed) (1959). *Arthurian Literature in the Middle Ages.* Oxford, Clarendon Press.

Lynch, Frances (1970). *Prehistoric Anglesey.* Angelsey.

McMahon, Brendan (2006). *The Princess who Ate People.* Wymeswold, Heart of Albion Press.

McMahon, Brendan (2009). *Cornish Folklore: The Nineteenth Century Background.* An Baner Kernewek.

MacCana, Proinsias (1968). *Celtic Mythology.* Reprinted (1996), London, Chancellor Press.

Mackenzie, Donald A. (1915). *Myths of Babylonia and Assyria.* London, Gresham.

MacKillop, James (1998). *Dictionary of Celtic Mythology.* Oxford, Oxford University Press.

BIBLIOGRAPHY

Malinowski, Bronisław (1926). "The Role of Myth in Life" in *Psyche*.

Marks, Shula, and Peter Richardson (eds) (1984). *International Labour Migration: Historical Perspectives*. Hounslow, Maurice Temple-Smith/ University of London.

Marris, Peter (1974). *Loss and Change, Reports of the Institute of Community Studies*. London, Routledge and Kegan Paul.

Marwick, Ernest W. (2000). *The Folklore of Orkney and Shetland*. Edinburgh, Birlinn.

Masson, Jeffrey M. (1985). *The Complete Letters of Sigmund Freud to Wilhelm Fliess 1887–1904*. Cambridge Ma, Harvard University Press.

Moore, A. W. (1891). *The Folklore of the Isle of Man*. Reprinted (1991), Llanerch.

Morrison, Sophia (1911). *Manx Fairy Tales*. London, David Nutt. Reprint (1971), Douglas, Manx Museum and National Trust.

Murdoch, Brian (1993). *Cornish Literature*. Cambridge, D S Brewer.

Murray Parkes, Colin (1972). *Bereavement: Studies of Grief in Adult Life*. London, Tavistock Publications. Reprint (1972), Harmondsworth, Penguin.

Nance, Robert Morton (1924). *Folk-lore Recorded in the Cornish Language (1924)*. 91st Annual Report of the Royal Cornwall Polytechnic Society, the author. Reprint (2000), Penzance, Oakmagic.

Nance, Robert Morton, and A. S. D. Smith (eds) (1966). *St Meriasek in Cornwall (Bewnans Meriasek)*. The Federation of Old Cornwall Societies.

Nicholson, Lewis E. (1963). *An Anthology of Beowulf Criticism*. Notre Dame, University of Notre Dame Press.

Norris, Edwin (1859). *The Ancient Cornish Drama*. Oxford, Oxford University Press.

Ó Cróinín, Dáibhí (2011). *Whitley Stokes 1830-1909. The Lost Celtic Notebooks Re-discovered*. Dublin. Four Courts Press.

Padel, Oliver J. (1975). *The Cornish Writings of the Boson Family*. Redruth, Institute of Cornish Studies.

Pascoe, W. H. (1985). *Teudar: A King of Cornwall*. Redruth, Truran.

Payton, Philip (1992). *The Making of Modern Cornwall: Historical Experience and the Persistence of Difference*. Redruth, Dyllansow Truran.

Payton, Philip (1996). *Cornwall*. Fowey, Alexander Associates. Revised edition (2004). *Cornwall: A History*. Fowey, Cornwall Editions.

Brendon, Piers (1975). *Hawker of Morwenstowe*. London, Cape.

Punter, David (1980). *The Literature of Terror*. London, Longman.

Purkiss, Diane (2000). *Troublesome Things: A History of Fairies and Fairy Stories*. London, Allen Lane. Reprinted (2007) as: *Fairies and Fairy Stories: A History*, London, Tempus Publishing.

Rappoport, Angelo S. (1928). *The Sea: Myths and Legends*. Reprinted (1995), London, Senate.

Rhys, John (1901). *Celtic Folklore, Volume 1: Welsh and Manx*. Oxford, Clarendon Press. Reprint (1980), London, Wildwood.

Rolt, L. T. C. (1970). *Victorian Engineering*. London, Allen Lane.

Rowe, John (1953). *Cornwall in the Age of the Industrial Revolution.* Liverpool, Liverpool University Press.

Rowse, A. L. (1941). *Tudor Cornwall: Portrait of a Society.* London, Jonathon Cape.

Rowse, A. L. (1986). *The Little Land of Cornwall.* London, Alan Sutton.

Saunders, Tim (1991). *The Wheel: An Anthology of Modern Poetry in Cornish 1850–1980.* London, Francis Boutle.

Schacker, Jennifer (2003). *National Dreams.* Philadelphia, University of Pennsylvania Press.

Seddon, Richard (1990). *The Mystery of Arthur at Tintagel.* London, Rudolf Steiner Press.

Simpson, Jacqueline, and Steve Roud (2000). *A Dictionary of English Folklore.* Oxford, Oxford University Press.

Spence, Lewis (1937). *Legendary London: Early London in Tradition and History.* London, Robert Hale and Co.

Spence, Lewis (1948). *The Minor Traditions of British Mythology.* London, Rider and Co.

Spence, Lewis (undated). *Legends and Romances of Brittany.* Reprinted (1997), New York, Dover.

Spooner, Barbara (1965). "The Giants of Cornwall" in *Folklore.* 76, §6–32.

Stern, Stephen, and John A. Cicala (eds) (1991). *Creative Ethnicity: Symbols and Strategies of Contemporary Ethnic Life.* Logan, Utah, Utah State University Press.

Stevens, Frank Leonard (1928). *Through Merrie England: The Pageantry and Pastimes of the Village and the Town.* London, Frederick Warne.

Stokes, Whitley (1864). *Guireans an bys. The Creation of the World.* London, Williams and Norgate.

Stokes, Whitley (1872). *The Life of St Meriasek, Bishop and Confessor.* London, Trübner.

Stoyle, Mark (2002). *West Britons: Cornish Identities and the Early Modern British State.* Exeter, University of Exeter.

Stoyle, Mark (2005). *Soldiers and Strangers: An Ethnic History of the English Civil War.*

Strachey, James (ed) (1917). *Complete Psychological Works of Sigmund Freud.* London, Hogarth Press.

Thomas, C. (1997). *See your own Country First: The Geography of a Railway Landscape.*

Thomas, Graham, and Nicholas Williams (eds) (2007). *Bewnans Ke: The Life of St Kea.* Exeter, University of Exeter Press.

Tomlin, E. W. F. (1982). *In Search of St Piran.* Padstow, Lodenek

Traill, David A. (1995). *Schliemann of Troy: Treasure and Deceit.* London, Penguin.

Warner, Marina (1994). *From the Beast to the Blond.* London, Chatto and Windus.

BIBLIOGRAPHY

Westland, Ella (1997). *Cornwall: The Cultural Construction of Place*. Penzance, Patten Press/University of Exeter.

Westwood, Jennifer (1987). *Albion: A Guide to Legendary Britain*. London, Paladin.

Westwood, Jennifer, and Jacqueline Simpson (2005). *The Lore of the Land*. London, Penguin.

Whetter, James (1988). *The History of Glasney College*. Padstow, Tabb House.

White, James F. (1962). *The Cambridge Movement: The Ecclesiologists and the Gothic Revival*. Cambridge, Cambridge University Press.

Wicker, Brian (1975). *The Story-Shaped World: Fiction and Metaphysics*. London, Athlone Press.

Williams, Derek R. (ed) (2004). *Henry and Katharine Jenner: A Celebration of Cornwall's Culture, Language and Identity*. London, Francis Boutle.

Williams, Nicholas, Michael Everson, and Alan M. Kent (2020). *The Charter Fragment and Pascon agan Arluth*. (Corpus Textuum Cornicorum; 1). Dundee: Evertype. ISBN 978-1-78201-182-8

Zaczek, Iain (2005). *Fairy Art, Artists and Inspirations*. London, Starfire Publishing.

Zimmermann, Georges Denis (2001). *The Irish Storyteller*. Dublin, Four Courts Press.

Zipes, Jack (ed) (2001). *The Oxford Companion to Fairy Tales*. Oxford, Oxford University Press.

Žižek, Slavoj (2008). *In Defence of Lost Causes*. London, Verso.

Index

INDEX

www.ingramcontent.com/pod-product-compliance
Lightning Source LLC
Chambersburg PA
CBHW030023290326
41934CB00005B/454